# Close Encounters
## with
## Twenty Israeli Writers

To Hanna

Interesting reading,

& let Negev

5-3-2003

# BOOKS OF RELATED INTEREST

The Arab in Hebrew Prose, 1911–1948
*Risa Domb*

Home Thoughts from Abroad: Distant Visions of Israel in
Contemporary Hebrew Fiction
*Risa Domb*

Look Up and Dream
*Robert Rietti*

The Man Who Liked Cats
*Edwin Samuel*

Myths in Israeli Culture: Captives of a Dream
*Nurith Gertz*

New Women's Writing from Israel
*Risa Domb*

Not of this Time, Not of this Place
*Yehuda Amichai*

The Old Country
*Sholom Aleichem*

One More River
*Lynne Reid Banks*

Set of Edge
*Bernice Rubens*

Tales of Old Sarajevo
*Isak Samokovlija*

The World is a Wedding
*Bernard Kops*

# Close Encounters
## with
# Twenty Israeli Writers

EILAT NEGEV

*Introduction by*
RISA DOMB

VALLENTINE MITCHELL
LONDON • PORTLAND, OR.

*First published in 2003 in Great Britain by*
VALLENTINE MITCHELL
Crown House, 47 Chase Side, Southgate
London N14 5BP

*and in the United States of America by*
VALLENTINE MITCHELL
c/o ISBS, 5824 N.E. Hassalo Street
Portland, Oregon, 97213-3644

*Website*: www.vmbooks.com

British Library Cataloguing in Publication Data

ISBN 0-85303-485-0 (cloth)
ISBN 0-85303-486-9 (paper)

Library of Congress Cataloging-in-Publication Data

A catalog record for this book is available
from the Library of Congress

Typeset in 11/13pt ClassGaramond by Vallentie Mitchell
Printed in Great Britain by MPG Books Ltd, Bodmin, Cornwall

*To Yehuda*

*For your love and inspiration*

# Contents

# *Preface*

'Don't mix up my underwear with that of my protagonist', novelist Amos Oz warned me, when a too-direct question threatened to penetrate the walls of secrecy that he had so laboriously built around himself throughout his life. But 'his underwear', so to speak, are scattered in his various novels: the suicide of Oz's mother, when he was just 12 and a half, and which had been hushed up, became a recurrent literary theme with him. Several of his protagonists, male or female, shared the same tragic element of a childhood scarred by an early, untimely death of a mother, and a life changed forever by the inability of the surviving parent to fill the void. It seemed as if Oz the novelist was taken over by the man Oz, forever reactivating his own trauma, unable to let his creations enjoy the love that was so brutally denied him.

It took Oz an entire lifetime, until in 2002, aged 62, he surprised all with *A Tale of Love and Darkness*, an autobiographical novel, where he revealed for the first time that, 'my mother ended her life in her sister's apartment in Ben Yehuda Street, Tel Aviv, on the night between Saturday and Sunday, 6 January 1952', and his exasperation at his inability to save her from her own hand. He wrote:

> About my mother I hardly ever spoke during my entire life, and up to now, up to the moment of writing these pages. Not with my father and not with my wife and not with my children and not with any soul on earth.

It was only through the format of a novel, that Oz could convey his personal tragedy to his family and friends, and to his readers. 'Every story that I ever wrote is autobiographical, no story is a confession', he confirmed in this book.

Having interviewed hundreds of writers in Israel and abroad, from Toni Morrison to Nadine Gordimer, Salman Rushdie and Paul Auster, I could not fail to see, every time, how each literary work carried in it a blueprint of the artist's life. As much as they try to explain their work as a figment of the imagination, they cannot conceal the personal veins that are buried inside like a network of subterranean routes, waiting to be discovered by a diligent excavator. So many themes and motifs, which go through the artist's complete body of work, can never be fully understood and their importance appreciated, without knowledge of his or her biography.

Israeli literature has all that, and an extra burden: the twentieth century being such a dramatic period in Jewish history, the personal biography is often archetypal, corresponding with the collective biography, and it all infiltrates and dominates the writing of Israeli authors.

With six million murdered, many Israelis are either Holocaust survivors, their offspring, or just citizens of a country which is so haunted by that trauma that it seems every military threat as another chapter in the Final Solution. Novelist Aharon Appelfeld, who was just eight years old when orphaned and deported, says: 'In every book I write, I revive my parents, my home town, my childhood. And beyond that, this is the story of an entire generation'. George Steiner described the first part of David Grossman's *See Under: Love* as 'one of the greatest achievements in the modern novel'. When Grossman explored the gradual awareness of the Holocaust, as perceived by an Israeli boy in the 1960s, he portrays his own growing awareness during the Eichmann trial in Jerusalem.

Poet Natan Zach, who was plucked from a prosperous, cultured home in Berlin as a child of five, still retains a markedly German accent 65 years later, and resembles so many others who were uprooted from Europe and never fully integrated into a harsh, unforgiving land. All, even Sabras (native Israelis), share some experience of immigration and absorption:

> If I were not aware of the gap between Ispahan and Kefar Saba, the tension between what my parents expected to find here, and what they found, I would probably not have become a writer. That is the pit out of which I write.

Says novelist, Dorit Rabinyan. She, like Ronit Matalon – both of them are daughters of immigrants from Iran and Egypt – expresses the sense of degradation and humiliation that hundreds of thousands of Sephardi Israelis have been feeling for decades; a humiliation that has made its way not only into the art, literature and academic life of modern Israel, but also into the voting ballot and into the Knesset.

In a country where every 18 year old is conscripted into the army, every writer has worn the khaki uniform, or is a parent of soldiers, and after seven wars in 54 years, it is no wonder that Israelis use them as landmarks to time personal events like graduation, marriage or the birth of a child. Bullets and blood pierce their writing, like that of novelist S. Yizhar, who had been a young officer in the War of Independence; or Meir Shalev, who was wounded by 'friendly fire' in 1967.

'The unliterary reality of the writer in Israel had become more real, fierce and prominent than his literary reality', novelist A.B. Yehoshua wrote in an essay after the Yom Kippur War of 1973. The devastation of that war, with over 2,700 dead, and a feeling of being let down by the military and political leadership, pushed writers into demonstrations, symposiums, the signing of petitions, and speaking in schools and army bases. 'Suddenly it became clear that the main battleground of the writers was not about books and literature, aesthetic problems or struggles between literary schools of thought, but about politics, social issues and issues of public morals'.

Looking at the biography of Virginia Wolf, Yehoshua wondered how she could have committed suicide in 1941, in England's Finest Hour. Although Wolf was very much concerned with the fate of her homeland, British solidarity did not abate her own loneliness. An Israeli writer (Yehoshua speculates) would probably not have committed suicide – since the sense of national solidarity, would diminish personal misery.

Literature is a popular pastime in Israel: 40 per cent of 'the People of the Book' claim to read at least one book a month; and 22 per cent list 'reading' as their main pastime, compared to 30 per cent who say it is watching television, and 8 per cent, going to the cinema. Around 5,000 new books are published in Israel each year, including around 700 novels, a considerable output for a nation, which has no more than five million Hebrew speakers.

From the onset of Zionism, men of letters held an indispensable and active role in the movement, and the dream of a Jewish state was first portrayed in a monograph, *Der Judenstadt*, by Theodore Herzl, who was a writer and journalist before coming the leader of the Zionist movement. In the parliament of the newly established State, 44 years after Herzl's death, writers like Uri-Zvi Greenberg, S. Yizhar and Moshe Shamir, have been elected on account of their spiritual standing. But more often than not, they turned out to be unsuitable for the political arena, being much better at fiction than at reality.

The horrors of the Second World War and the struggle for independence inspired poet Natan Alterman to discard a successful career of lyrical poetry and to switch to political writing. For 24 years, his weekly newspaper column commented, in rhyme, on major milestones in the making of Israel. An avid reader of the poet, Prime Minister David Ben-Gurion, was aware of the poet's public influence, tolerated his sharp arrows and did not criticize him openly. In November 1948, Alterman's column portrayed a young soldier careering through the streets of an occupied town in his jeep, joy-shooting an old Arab; Ben-Gurion had the poem printed and distributed to all army units.

In later years, politicians turned their back on writers, but the public still harks to them. 'Standing on an abyss, the need for a prophet rises, and the writer has the appropriate qualifications', A.B. Yehoshua cynically comments: 'verbal skills, a good usage of metaphors, a certain sense of abstraction, and a small personal neurosis'. The media, newspapers and television alike, regularly call on them to put into words public sentiments when at national crossroads.

When poet Natan Zach travels on a train, people gather around him. 'They think a poet, especially if he also appears on television, is some sort of a minor guru, even if he doesn't cast out demons, sprinkle holy water or give you rabbit's urine to drink'.

In the twentieth century, Jews have undergone a process of secularisation, which has become more explicit in modern Israel. Rabbis and religious leaders have lost their centrality as path setters, and writers and poets have taken their place. The poems of Yehuda Amichai have become secular prayers, a substitute for those who feel that the Jewish prayer book does not express their emotions. His poems are printed on wedding invitations, read as vows under the bridal canopy, and even more so, recited in funerals, over the open grave. 'I write about my life, about love, bearing children, about loss, and people find themselves in me', he once told me. An Israeli living in New York, who read in Amichai's poem: 'don't love/those from far away. Take yourself one/from nearby./ The way a sensible house will take local/stones for its' building,' left his American fiancée and returned to Israel to marry his former girlfriend.

When I interviewed Ted Hughes in October 1996, he expressed his envy at this role. The British Poet Laureate said that in England poets have no moral weight and the only thing that their public wants is entertainment.

In socialist Israel, it was thought egotistical to put oneself in the centre. In a country still living by the sword, it is no wonder that the first biographies to appear were of military men and politicians. There are hardly any biographies of writers, and *Close Encounters*, offering 20 short ones, is a humble step towards filling this void.

I have consulted academics who teach Hebrew Literature in

British and American universities, so that the book will include the more prominent writers, those who are also known outside Israel, and have been more widely translated into English than others.

*Close Encounters* is arranged chronologically, from the oldest to the most recent, attempting to cover a hundred years of Israeli literature. The change of style and subject matter hints at the demographical and historical transformations that have occurred during that span of time. The profiles are based on interviews that I carried out with all the living writers, or – in the case of deceased ones – with family members, biographers and researchers. In a century of growing female importance, it is no coincidence that among the first five writers represented in this book, all of whom were born around the turn of the twentieth century, there are four men and only one woman (the poetess Leah Goldberg); while in the last five, the ratio is completely reversed, with four women and only one man, the novelist David Grossman.

In the early days of the State, Jaffa oranges were the pride export of Israel; and then came diamonds; and, nowadays, it is books. Translations of Israeli prose enjoy an unusual prominence, much more than other literatures of comparably small countries. It may be due to the interest in the Holy Land, or to its unfortunate recurrence in the news. In some European countries, they even dominate the bestseller lists. Meir Shalev's novels are a big hit in Holland, and Zeruya Shalev's *Love Life* and *Husband and Wife* sold over 100,000 copies each in Germany – more than either did in Israel. It may be a symptom of guilt, or curiosity, about that section of society which was so cruelly and totally plucked from their culture 60 years ago; a desire to see what the children of those Jews are producing now, from afar.

Israelis are going through dramatic, turbulent events; experiencing an existential, social and religious crisis. This intense life means that Israelis occupy several layers of existence, which create many kinds of personal experiences that writers in other countries seldom experience. Thus, a reading of the writers' profiles offers a different way of viewing Israel, since each writer has taken part in events outside his or her own personal scope. All this becomes subject matter, and their writing creates a wide panorama not just of literature but also of Israeli life.

*Eilat Negev*
*Jerusalem*
*2003*

# Introduction:
# Israeli Literature in Fifty Years of Statehood

Israeli literature is part of a continuous literary corpus, called
Modern Hebrew literature, which extends beyond fixed
geographical boundaries. Modern Hebrew literature emerged not
in Israel but in Europe over 200 years ago, at the time when Jewish
life began to emerge from its seclusion and reach out towards
Western culture. Along with European Humanism, Modern
Hebrew literature shifted its vision from God to Man and became
secular, giving rise to the movement of Jewish Enlightenment
(1781–1881). This movement, which began in Prussia as a rational-
ist movement, had assumed a romantic-nationalistic aspect by the
middle of the nineteenth century, as the major Jewish cultural
centres shifted from Western to Eastern Europe. The wave of
pogroms that struck Russian Jewry in the 1880s undermined the
possibility of the ideal of Jewish emancipation in Europe and indi-
rectly initiated the Zionist movement. This brought about yet
another geographical shift. The various waves of Jewish immigra-
tions finally moved the Hebrew cultural centre from Europe to the
Holy Land, or Palestine as it was then called. Thus, it is only since
1948, with the establishment of the State of Israel, that Israeli, as
opposed to Hebrew or Jewish, literature came into being.

The story of Israeli literature runs in parallel with that of the
State of Israel, and both are identical with the story of Zionism.
The Zionist dream, conceived in the darker days of European
Jewish history, was fulfilled with the movement of Jews, albeit in
relatively small numbers, from West to East: from an exilic existence in Europe, to a more settled life in a homeland in the Holy
Land, in Eretz Israel. Idealism and national aspirations in the
context of unexpectedly harsh reality are the hallmarks of Hebrew
literature of that period of time, the period immediately preceding
the establishment of the State of Israel. The Biblical Hebrew

language, which was revived and adapted to become a living, spoken language, demonstrates a unique link between language and Jewish identity. In our own times, nationalism can be seen as the most significant new (or revived) factor of Jewish identity and the Hebrew language as its emblem.

The first generation of Hebrew writers, the so-called '1948-generation', who wrote directly after the establishment of the State of Israel, was no longer dominated by immigrants, but mainly by native Hebrew speakers, or by Sabras, the native-born Israelis. These writers – such as Yizhar, Aharon Meged, Nathan Shaham and Moshe Shamir – were consciously parochial and they, as well as their protagonists, shared a collective biography: members in a Zionist youth movement, life on a kibbutz, tilling the land, and in many cases ultimately sacrificing their life in a war defending their country. Their shared experience is well represented in their writings, but in addition to this, there is one particular theme, which constantly preoccupied them, and that is the portrayal of the Arab in their writings.

Ever since their very first meeting with the Arabs at the turn of the century, Hebrew writers to a greater or lesser extent strove to depict the Arab in their works. Initially, for obvious cultural reasons, they portrayed the Arabs from a patronising, superior viewpoint and at the same time described a sentimentalised notion of friendly relations, even brotherhood. With the establishment of the State of Israel, the writers addressed themselves to a consideration of the ethical problems arising from a state of war, particularly S. Yizhar in *Days of Ziklag*. Remarkably, they gave a voice to the enemy. I know of no other parallel case in the history of contemporary literature. However, with the borders closed until June 1967, Israeli literature became a literature of siege. In particular in Amos Oz and A.B. Yehoshua, the Arab was no longer a concrete individual but an abstract, a symbol, which was often associated with the sexual attraction of forbidden fruit, a nightmare which worried them and which they could not and did not wish to ignore. The portrayal of the Arab changed once again with the trauma of the 1973 war. From that point the Arab was no longer an abstract idea, a threat, but a concrete man of flesh and blood. Israeli writers like David Grossman continue today to re-evaluate their attitude to Arabs in the light of ever-changing social, political, economic and psychological conditions.

After the realisation of the basic Zionist dream, the foundation of the State of Israel, and after the euphoria in the wake of independence, when the Zionist dream was institutionalised in statehood, the hitherto apparent cohesiveness of society began to be shaken. Israeli identity was no longer unified and monolithic. Up to 1967 only one voice was heard: Ashkenazi, male, socialist, secular and politically identified with the Left. In their attempt to break away from this, some writers turned from the social realism of their predecessors to universalism and psychological archetypes. This phase did not last long, and it has been suggested that this stance 'was not a rejection of ideology *per se*, but rather a challenge to and a critique of the particular norms, both aesthetic and ideological, of the previous generation' – to quote Professor Yael Feldman of New York University. As a result of disillusionment, the so-called 'New Wave' – a term coined by Professor Gershon Shaked of the Hebrew University – literature of the 1960s and 1970s expressed alienation from society and shifted its vision from the collective to the individual. The early parochial approach and dissociation of the Sabra generation of 1948 from European culture was revived again in this period, when writers turned once more towards Western literature, feeling that the actual geographical limits to their fictional world had restricted the imagination of their predecessors. This view coincided with the political and economic circumstances, which enabled Israeli writers to travel abroad more easily. The renewed encounter with Europe triggered admiration and attraction as well as hostility and repulsion. Some protagonists escape to Europe and others from Europe, but in both cases Europe never serves as just a tourist's sightseeing spot abroad but as a world which stands in total contrast to Israel. It is much easier to ask fundamental questions about the nature of the whole Israeli enterprise when placing the fictional characters afar. Distance serves not so much the purpose of discovering the 'Other', as of examining the self.

The Modernism and Existentialism that dominated European literature (such as in the writings of Kafka, Camus, Becket and Ionesco) suited the mode of expression of these writers. They expressed ambivalence and irony and portrayed marginal, displaced, characters using the pathetic and tragic together with the grotesque and with parody. These writers reacted against their predecessors and strove to move away from rationality towards universalism and from reflecting the problems of the community to reflecting those of the individual. They also sought to free themselves from the influence of the Russian literary tradition. This had lain heavily upon Hebrew literature ever since its flourishing phase in Russia prior to its move to Eretz Israel. Nevertheless, Israeli writers inherited the Russian tradition of their predecessors in regarding literature as a tool to promote national and social ideologies. As Amos Oz once commented:

> Israel is probably the only country in the world where an editorial in a major paper picks an argument with a fictitious character ... Many non-Israeli writers may envy us for having such a historical tail wind as we write, but there is a high price to pay for this intense interest in literature: the writer is ascribed the role of prophet and is treated accordingly.

The experience of war had naturally been the main theme that occupied the literature of the first generation of Hebrew writers in the newly established Israel. Still feeling the responsibility to help shape their society, they glorified heroism and comradeship. During that period, women's writing, and particularly prose, was scarce. It has been suggested that women could not reflect any of these immediate Israeli preoccupations in their writing, as they were beyond their personal experience. Whether or not this was the case, their writing was peripheral to the central experience of the country.

This has changed since the 1960s. The trend in Israeli fiction of the New Wave, of giving marginal characters centre stage, as well as the exploration of themes other than the largely male-orientated national concerns, opened the doors to an influx of women writers such as Hannah Bat-Shahar, Orly Castel-Bloom, Yehudit Katzir and Savyon Liebrecht. The change in mainstream Israeli experience meant greater openness in literature, and a pluralism of voices emerged, incorporating those of women writers. As a result, women could, at last, abandon their traditional (non-) place in Hebrew literature and assume their rightful role in its development. With the generation of the New Wave of the 1960s and 1970s, women's prose writing at last found its niche.

The relationship between ever-changing generations of writers is particularly interesting in the development of Israeli literature and is reflected in fictional writings. It has been suggested that the Zionist-Modernist narrative reflects Oedipal rebellion: on the one hand the protagonists are faithful to the Founding Fathers' generation, and on the other, they are aware that this endangers their existence as individuals – as in early works by Amos Oz and A.B. Yehoshua.

One criticism of the Founding Fathers has often been expressed through the metaphor of the binding of Isaac. More recently, a new development on this issue was represented: the Founding

Fathers were no longer providing role models or a sense of security for children riveted with anxiety about decoding the adult world, fighting the shadows of that world, and worrying about whether they would be able to function sexually in the adult realm – as in David Grossman's, *The Book of Intimate Grammar*. Interestingly, these near-universal worries of children and young adults the world over demonstrate that Israeli preoccupations were at last falling more into line with those of the wider world.

The literature of the 1970s, which witnessed the advent of voices that had not been heard before, also expressed the Holocaust experience. The prolonged silence on the Israeli literary scene in response to the Holocaust was broken as a result of the Eichman trial in 1961. This public event generated a tremendous response as it allowed survivors to testify, bringing to Israeli consciousness what they had experienced. It was then that Aharon Appelfeld began publishing his fiction about the Holocaust. Since that time, his has been the most sustained and acclaimed treatment of the subject. The treatment of the Holocaust in Hebrew literature in prose, poetry and drama, continues to develop. The lengthening perspective of time gives Israeli writers, mainly the second and third generations of survivors, a new position. Professor Avner Holtzman, from Tel Aviv University, noted that, 'The ageing and dwindling of survivors and witnesses means the Holocaust is changing from the active, painful personal experience of living people to a distant historical memory'. The poetic solutions which these writers propose are the realistic depictions of the echoes of the Holocaust in current Israeli life, the new form of artistic-documentary writing, and the post-modernist approach. These directions are incorporated in Grossman, *See Under: Love*. No doubt future generations will continue to portray this historical event, which has become part of the national collective memory.

In 1977 the Likud party, led by Menahem Begin, came into power, with the large Sephardi constituency coming into its own. This was a turning point. It signalled even greater pluralism. Writers of 'Oriental', or 'Sephardi', origin began to express pride in their roots and to reflect the societies to which they had belonged before their immigration to Israel. Several authors, like Dan Benayah Serry, Sami Michael, Eli Amir, Ronit Matalon and Dorit Rabinyan, focussed on the Oriental Jewish community in their different countries of origin. In addition, through fictionalised autobiographical retrospectives, writers' ideological disorientation prompted a re-evaluation of their own social and political standing. Having identified themselves as Israelis, they now became Israeli Jews. It has been suggested that as the secular Israeli Jew moves away from the original Zionist models, so the literature becomes increasingly contemplative and preoccupied with the problem of identity. Hebrew writing has come a long way from the myth of the New Jew in the early settlement, to the undermining of the myth of the Sabra in the post-modern and post-Zionist Israeli literature of the late 1980s and early 1990s, as in Meir Shlev's novel *The Blue Mountain*, which describes how the Zionist project of the pioneering fathers is turned into a place of burial for Jews from the Diaspora.

The 1980s was probably the most prolific period in the development of the literature of the State of Israel, of prose in particular. The Lebanon War, at the beginning of the decade, and the war of the Intifada, at the end, aroused heated political controversies, which in turn were reflected in contemporary literature. Many contemporary prose writers are once again exploring the past, in particular the life of the early settlers. Israeli literature seemed to yearn towards the lost paradise of the early settlements rather than seeking to propose a new one. Utopia for them is the reality of the past, whereas the present is nothing but a great and ugly dystopia. But, as S. Yizhar suggested:

> Perhaps there is no Utopia in an open society, which succeeds in withstanding more than three generations: the founders' generation that undertook a mission, the generation of the sons, which internalised but also began to show some reservations, and the third generation, which no longer saw itself committed to the original dreams, and which occasionally even chose to draw away not only from the dreams but also from the place of the dreamers. Some explain the decline of Utopia as a reaction to all the wars in which Isaac was required to be sacrificed for Abraham's faith, war after war as historical landmarks branded like painful burns in every personal biography.

The writings of the 1980s are highly political, reacting directly to the political, the ideological and the social reality. Whereas this was unacceptable to the poetic consensus of the 1960s, the involvement of the authors and their works in the political arena during the 1970s, and more so during the 1980s, was embraced and made aesthetically legitimate. Both the critics and the reading public accepted and expected this mode of writing. The change is particularly discernible in the characterisation of the protagonists. They are Israelis who struggle with specific Israeli problems rather than anonymous characters that struggle with universal existential problems.

The literary scene in Israel changed dramatically in the 1990s. Recent years have witnessed a new phenomenon: some books appeared in which the centre is not the Zionist narrative, but the Jewish community in Europe before and after the Second World War. This is reminiscent of S.Y. Agnon's earlier writing. The only Israeli writer to have received a Nobel Prize for literature, in 1966, Agnon portrayed mainly the lives of lost European Jewry rather than life in Eretz Israel. An even more dramatic development is the appearance for the first time in Israeli writing of street language from young Israeli writers suspicious of 'literary language' with its allusions to the Bible, the Talmud and other traditional Jewish sources. There is also an abundance of short short collections written by 19- to 23-year-old writers, clearly aimed at young readers. It seems that the Israeli book market is so hungry for new voices that major publishing houses are keen to accept even young and inexperienced writers. It has been noted that there are also several Orthodox or ex-Orthodox women writers. Interestingly, most voices that come out of the religious society are female, like novelists Hannah Bat-Shahar and Mira Magen and poet Haia-Esther. Orthodox women read more, so they can write freely, while the husbands, confined to the Yeshiva, have poor command of Modern Hebrew, and in any case consider anything outside their *Gemara* studies as a waste of time.

Despite the multitude of voices emanating from the generation of the 1980s and 1990s, the object of their confrontation is still more often than not the Zionist text. As Natan Shaham reminds us: 'Zionism is the only successful revolution of the twentieth century'. The Zionist text remains the one spiritual presence with which these writers interact, loading it with new meanings from the Israeli experience as they perceive and experience it. The main themes in many contemporary writings are Zionist and Sabra ideologies. Questioning and examining the two lead to another theme, which is the search for the self, particularly *vis-à-vis* Jewish identity.

*Dr Risa Domb*
*Faculty of Oriental Studies, University of Cambridge*
*2002*

# CHAPTER ONE

# Shmuel-Yosef Agnon
## (1887–1970)

# Abandoned People, Lost Places

As a result of the historic catastrophe, in which Titus of Rome destroyed Jerusalem, and Israel was exiled from its land, I was born in one of the cities of the Exile, but always I regarded myself as one who was born in Jerusalem.

Thus spoke Shmuel-Yosef Agnon in his acceptance speech for the Nobel Prize for literature in 1966, of the load of history on his shoulders. No wonder that, decades before, upon arrival in Palestine, he declared that he was born on the Ninth of Av, 8 August 1888. No one noticed at the time that the discrepancy between the Hebrew and Gregorian calendars made the coinciding of the two dates impossible; the Ninth of Av, a fast marking the destruction of the First and Second Temple, fell three weeks earlier in that year, on 17 July 1888. Agnon's official birth certificate states a different year altogether: 8 August 1887. He was probably trying to catch three birds in one throw: to have a Jewish historical birth-date, with only one repeated digit, and also, make himself younger by a year.

'With a great writer, in order to fathom the depths of his soul, one has to examine not only his biography, but the stories he invents about himself', says Professor Arnold Band of UCLA, a leading Agnon scholar:

Imagination and reality were one and the same for Agnon, and just as he created a world for his heroes, so he wanted to tailor a reality for himself; it was this ambition that made him a great storyteller. According to tradition, the Ninth of Av marks the beginning of 2000 years of Jewish Exile and also the day on which the Messiah was destined to be born. Did Agnon think of himself as the Messiah? Why not? After all, every Jew has Messianic aspirations.

He was born Shmuel-Yosef Czaczkes, the eldest of five children, in the Galician town of Buczacz, then in the Austro-Hungarian Empire, now in Poland. His father had rabbinical training, but was a prosperous fur trader. Shmuel-Yosef was raised in mixed cultures; he learned the scriptures from his father, and German literature from his mother. They became his main mentors when he completed his formal schooling at the age of ten. Free to wander and do whatever took his fancy, he was widely read, his favourites being Ibsen and Knut Hamsun.

'When I was nine years old, I wrote a ballad about a boy who goes down to the river, to light candles on the first day of the Selihoth, for penitential prayers, and a water nymph emerged from the water and takes him away', wrote Agnon to the critic Zak:

> That was my second poem, after a poem of longing for my father that I wrote when he went away on his travels. From then on I was like an inexhaustible fountain, every day I would write a long, horrifying poem.

'Thank goodness not a single syllable of my childhood poems survived', he added, with characteristically acute self-criticism.

'My forebears and I are of the ministers that were in the Temple', said Agnon in his Stockholm speech. In his nightly visions he saw himself singing in the Holy Temple, but:

> I suspect that the angels in charge of the Shrine of Music, fearful lest I sing in wakefulness what I had sung in dream, made me forget by day what I had sung at night ... to console me for having prevented me from singing with my mouth, they enabled me to compose songs in writing.

In 1908, he gave the writer and editor Simcha Ben-Zion the manuscript of *Agunot* [Abandoned Wives]. 'Ben-Zion agreed to publish it but said Czaczkes was a ridiculous surname, and insisted that the author change it', says Professor Band. 'All his life Agnon wrote about people who were literally and spiritually abandoned. He understood that modern man has no freedom and no home. That is why he chose the name Agnon, derived from *Agunot*.'

His future as a Hebrew writer was already clear to him, and he saw no point in remaining in Boczacz, and that same year he immigrated to Palestine, not least to avoid conscription into the Austro-Hungarian Army. He declared that he wished 'to till its soil and live by the labour of my hands', but the only work he could find was clerical, as Secretary of the Jewish Magistrate Court in Jaffa.

In 1912 he returned to Berlin to study literature. When the Great War broke out, he feared being conscripted into the German Army. 'He decided to disable himself for military service', says Professor Dan Laor from the Tel Aviv University, and Agnon's biographer:

He began smoking heavily, drank huge quantities of coffee and cut down severely on his sleeping hours. His health degenerated considerably and he was temporarily exempted. The price was dear, a kidney disease which cost him five months in a hospital. During this period he met the publisher Zalman Schocken, who became his patron and freed him from financial worries and enabled him to devote his time to writing.

His relationship with women was complex. 'They attracted and frightened him at the same time', says Dr Nitsa Ben-Dov from the University of Haifa:

His male heroes wait for their women to come on a white horse and hand them the flower of their maidenhood. They are fascinated by women, but in order to fight attraction, they search for faults; they declare that she is frigid, or promiscuous, or fickle-headed, and the self-fulfilling prophesy breaks the relationship down.

It was different with Esther Marx. In a family of 11 children, several of whom became scholars and professors, Esther, born in 1889, was an outstanding personality. 'She was a brilliant, modern woman', says her daughter, Emuna Yaron:

At an early age she left for Munich to study art, later she went to Palestine to visit her sister and when she returned to Germany she began learning Arabic. It was unconventional for a girl from a good family to show such independence. Agnon came to her father's home, to teach him Hebrew, and fell in love with her on the spot. Since Esther was of a higher social status than Agnon, her father was wary of the relationship, and refused to attend the wedding. Only later, when he came to realize that his son-in-law was a genius, did he come to terms with the match and even help them financially.

The bride was 31, the groom 32. Emuna was born in 1921 and her brother Hemdat 14 months later.

'Without her, I would have perished', said Agnon in a radio interview. 'But I did have problems, every man has problems with his wife. When the Almighty wanted to punish a part of humanity, he gave them wives'.

Love in Agnon's works is a complex, convoluted emotion; most of his male protagonists are passive, incapable of loving or relating to a woman, while the women are always on the go. 'He writes about men who seek intimacy, but are inhibited by their love for their mother', says Professor Band. 'Agnon loved his mother dearly and may have harboured guilt towards her, as he left home for Palestine in 1908, when she was seriously ill and died soon after'. *In the Prime of her Life* begins with the words, 'My mother died in the prime of her life'. The daughter in the story, Tirza, married her mother's former lover, a forbidden relationship bordering on incest, which was a recurrent theme with Agnon.

'Like Flaubert, who said, "I am Emma Bovary", Agnon could say, "I am Tirza"', says Dr Nitsa Ben-Dov. '*In the Prime of her Life* is a spiritual autobiography. Tirza prays for a daughter who will fill her husband's every need. Agnon was a psychological novelist, well versed in the secret depths of the soul, alert to such subtleties of feeling'.

A fire in the Agnon home in Bad Homburg consumed his rare collection of 4,000 Hebrew books, and all his manuscripts, including 700 pages of his unpublished novel, ironically named *Eternal Life*. Agnon interpreted this as divine punishment for his prolonged stay in the Diaspora. In October 1924, he moved to Jerusalem, to prepare the way for his wife and children. This was the first in a long series of separations, during which they wrote each other almost daily. Their daughter Emuna found the letters after their death and published them in *My Darling Esther*:

> In one of his letters he described a visit to a house in Jerusalem, 'and as soon as I uttered my name, a woman with two children immediately appeared and asked me to sign my name on one of my books. When she couldn't find the book, because she had lent it to someone, she picked up a Bible and said: "Sign here!" I said to her: "Madame, I'm not the author of this book"'.

Agnon's great popularity made him a favourite with women, and he did not spare his wife any jealousy:

> When the women shake my hand in greeting, they hold on to it. But I don't pay any attention. I think only of you...I have a request to make of you, my darling, do exercises every day, lest you grow fat, God forbid!

He criticized her letter ... full of mistakes, both stylistic and in spelling, which made it hard to understand. 'Estherlein, I realize that you wrote the letter in a hurry. Do you really have no time for your husband, living so far away and waiting every week for a letter from you?' But, most of all, he strongly opposed her plan to be a gymnastics teacher:

> If you take my advice, you will study gymnastics just for yourself and for the children. If you are looking for work, you can find it with me. What can I say? I'm an old-fashioned man, I do not think that women have to earn a living; it is enough for the husband to support the family. Leave paid employment for the unmarried old maids, may God have mercy on them, who are hungry and cannot find work.

He described the hardships of Palestine, to discourage Esther from coming:

> There are no servant-girls here in the European sense. Anyone who takes a Yemenite, Bukharan or Persian woman into his house will have to teach her over and over again until he himself gets used to all the dirt in the house. When I see how much

women have to suffer here, I become very concerned for our future.

Esther was offended:

> Just like the last time, several months ago, you are getting very nervous about my arrival. Your last letter proved to me that this cannot go on. For the last ten months you have had things relatively easy. I suggest that now, when I get to the Land of Israel with the children, we live apart, you will have the peace and quiet you find comfortable and I will have the children. Living on closer terms – or so I understand from your anxiety – will not be good for either of us ... You are right; I cannot fulfil the role of your wife. I love you very much, more than anyone else, but I have been forced to acknowledge that this is not enough for us to live together.

The threat of a divorce had its effect, and in late 1925, after a year of separation, Esther Agnon came to Jerusalem with her children. 'Relationships between artists and their wives are a central theme with Agnon', says Dr Ariel Hirschfeld from the Hebrew University:

> Agnon took the grim aspect of the Orpheus myth, the artist-husband who turns his wife into his Muse and later brings about her death. *Abandoned Wive's* protagonist lures the woman like a spider lures a fly, turns her into an artistic creation and then neglects her. *The Tale of the Scribe*, which Agnon dedicated to his wife, deals with a writer who authors books instead of siring children, he and his wife live a life of abstinence, they never touch each other, and only after her death does he succeed in writing. In other words, the artist brings about his wife's death and turns her into an object of yearning and desire.

Emuna Yaron remembers that throughout her life her mother had to fight for independence, as Agnon wanted her all to himself and sabotaged every opportunity she had for a career of her own.

Agnon made use of every scrap of paper. Sometimes he would take envelopes and cut them open, writing on the blank side, not stopping at wedding invitations and theatre tickets. Between the lines he left a space for his numerous corrections. For 40 years, his wife would type out his incomprehensible, dense handwriting:

It was a labour of love, and he placed her under great pressure. No matter how much of a perfectionist she was and made demands upon herself, he was never satisfied. Sometimes she had typed the same page four times, over and over, since each time he introduced more corrections. She was bitter, but at the same time argued in his defence: that he worked hard and did not have much pleasure in life. She wouldn't let any other woman replace her, not even my sister, and preferred that I should do it ...

Says the son, Hemdat Agnon.

'Agnon is a difficult subject for a biographer, since his main activity was writing and there were no great dramas in his life', says Professor Dan Laor:

For 40 years he lived in the same house, married to the same woman. Unlike other writers he did not engage in political activity, signed no petitions and, apart from one occasion when he supported the Movement for a Greater Land of Israel, he did not take part in public affairs. He chose to live in Jerusalem, far from the madding crowd, whereas most of the writers were secular and lived in Tel Aviv.

His home in Talpiot was austerely furnished, without curtains or armchairs, only folding chairs. His study was filled with books and he wrote leaning against a rostrum for hours at a time. When he was tired, he would stand on a bottle, as recommended by a physical training teacher. 'Father was a famous author, much in demand, and everything at home had to be done quietly. We cried quietly, we even quarrelled quietly', says his daughter:

Father was very attached to me. He didn't like my boyfriends, and was dismayed. He said I was to devote several years to him as his secretary, and only then would be able to live my own life. I wasn't prepared to do that, and felt bitterly resentful. Only after he died did I begin to understand him more and become closer to him. Today, perhaps I am too much involved in his life and writings than is desirable.

When Agnon was a boy and was studying the rules for ritual slaughtering, his father took him to an abattoir. From that day on he never touched meat. He came from a ritually observant family, but was ambivalent: he attended the synagogue, but was engaged in an inner struggle. He seemed to be wrestling with faith, striving with all his heart to believe with perfect faith. Esther, who was not observant, was obliged to keep a kosher home for him. She was in awe with him, but on Shabbat she used earphones to listen secretly to the radio in her room. Agnon pretended not to know, accepting it as long as she did not do it in public; appearances were more important to him than observing the prohibitions in full.

Tirza, the heroine of *In the Prime of her Life*, is miserable that her husband, Akabia, is too much absorbed in his art: 'He really was born to be a bachelor, why did I rob him of his peace and quiet', pregnant Tirza torments herself as she sits outside the locked room where her husband is writing his book. 'I would willingly die, for I have been a stumbling block to Akabia. Night and day I pray to God to give me a daughter and let her tend to all his needs'.

There were times when Esther Agnon could no longer bear living in the company of her husband. 'She still preserved remnants of the great love she felt for him and she admired his talent, but she never managed to come to terms with his egocentricity, his autocratic nature, especially the offensive, painful way he treated her', says Professor Dan Laor:

> Esther Agnon was beautiful, clever and well bred and won the respect of all who met her, but this did not prevent her husband from humiliating her in the presence of strangers. 'Can you believe it, once she was beautiful', he once asked the guests at a party, pointing at her. He needed her but her presence distressed him and disturbed his privacy. However, when she went away for extended periods to be with her sister, he sent her long pleading letters. When the separations lengthened, he would fear she had decided to part from him, an idea he found intolerable.

Agnon loved to hear gossip and stories about people and use it as raw material for his stories. Professor Arnold Band met Agnon several times a week during the two years of writing *Nostalgia and Nightmare* (1968); a study of Agnon's life and work.

Each time he would question me about what I had been doing since we last met. I would tell him something and a week later he would tell me a wonderful story, about something that had happened to him, exactly the same incident as I had told him the week before. I would say to him, 'Mr Agnon, it didn't happen to you, it happened to me', and he would say: 'That's not true. What are you talking about?' At first I would be angry, how could he take over my story and put it to his own use? Then I understood, and once I had understood, I found the key to his personality. It wasn't my story, it had merely happened to me. Agnon took my small, unimportant anecdote and turned it into a wonderful story of which he was the hero.

Agnon's longest novel – 600 pages – *The Bridal Canopy*, which appeared in 1931, paid homage to the religious Jewish life in Poland. But Agnon was not only recording reminiscences from a world left behind. The protagonists of his greatest novel – *Only Yesterday* – were immigrants trying to carve themselves a new life in Palestine.

His last novel, *Shira,* which he wrote intermittently over 20 years, 'is the greatest novel of infidelity in Hebrew literature', says Dr Nitsa Ben-Dov:

The hero, Herbst, meaning 'autumn' in German, is in the autumn of his life. A married family man, he falls in love with a nurse at the hospital where his wife is about to give birth. The wife resembles Agnon's own Esther, while the mistress, Shira, is plain, masculine, wearing trousers, a feminist who left her husband when she realized he was inadequate. She excites Herbst with stories of her sado-masochistic relations with another man who lashes her with a whip. Herbst has two grown-up daughters, Zohara is beautiful and feminine as her mother, and Tamara is rebellious and masculine as Shira. There is a hint of incest about Herbst's relationship with Shira.

At the end of the story Herbst leaves his wife and joins Shira who, in the meantime, has fallen ill with leprosy. They achieve a genuine bond only in the leper colony, on the brink of death. 'In all of Agnon's stories there is an unrealised desire to pursue true love', says Dr Ben-Dov. 'It was comfortable for Agnon to have a wife who served him, but as a writer he was attracted to the independent feminist, with whom life would be a sexual, emotional and intellectual challenge'.

In 1966 Agnon was awarded the Nobel Prize for Literature. He felt
that the prize had come too late and was disgruntled at having to
share it with the Jewish poet Nelly Sachs. 'At my age they saddle me
with a concubine', he complained.

In the middle of 1969, nine months before he died, Agnon fell
ill and remained paralysed on his left side. He lost his speech, but
his mind was lucid. During this period his daughter was editing
*Shira*. Whenever in doubt as to the final version of a sentence or
choice of words, she would place before him two or three possible
interpretations of what he had written and he would put his finger
on what he thought was correct.

On the last night of his life he was rushed to hospital, the team
of doctors and nurses standing around him, he pointed to his head,
indicating that he wanted to wear his skullcap. He placed it on his
head and in a loud voice cried out the prayer *Shema Yisrael* ('Hear,
O Israel, the Lord our God, the Lord is One'). On 17 February
1970, he passed away. His wife Esther died three years later.


## TRANSLATIONS INTO ENGLISH

Agnon, S.-Y., *A Guest for the Night* [*Ore'ach Nata La'lun*] (New
    York: Schocken Books, 1968).
—— *Two Tales: Betrothed, and Edo and Enam* [*Shvu'at Emunim
    and Edo ve-Einam*] (Harmondsworth: Penguin Books, 1971).
—— *Twenty-One Stories* [this contains *In the Prime of her Life*
    (*Bidmi* Yameah) trans. N. Kozodoy] (New York: Schocken
    Books, 1989).
—— *Shira* [trans. Z. Shapiro] (New York: Schocken Books, 1989).
—— *A Book that Was Lost And Other Stories* [*Sefer she'Avad*; trans.
    A.G. Hoffman] (New York: Schocken Books, 1995).
—— *Days of Awe* [*Yamim Norayim*; trans. Maurice T. Galpert]
    (New York: Schocken Books, 1995).
—— *A Simple Story* [*Sipur Pashut*; trans. H. Halkin]  (New York:
    Syracuse University Press, 1999).
——*The Bridal Canopy* [*Hakhnasat Kala*; trans. I.M.Lask] (New
    York: Syracuse University Press, 2000).
—— *Only Yesterday* [*Temol Silsham*; trans. B. Harshav] (Princeton,
    NJ: Princeton University Press, 2000).

# CHAPTER TWO

# Uri-Zvi Greenberg
## (1896–1981)

# Eyes that Penetrate the Abyss

The first time Aliza saw Uri-Zvi Greenberg, she couldn't fail to notice how bloodshot his green eyes were. He seemed to be pausing between one bout of weeping and the next. This was in 1949, and the newly married Jerusalemite, ex-member of the right-wing underground group Lehi, paid a visit with two girlfriends to their much-admired poet and spiritual inspiration. She had read his *Book of Denunciation and Faith* and wished to be acquainted with the writer of what (she felt) was the absolute truth. 'Facing him, I got the impression that he had extraordinary powers of concentration, his eyes turned inwards'.

For many years Uri-Zvi Greenberg remained a bachelor, an ascetic, and did not seek the love of a woman. He lived in an inner world of nightmares. 'Why did God give me reason, golden hair on my head, and eyes that penetrate the abyss, to the depths of disaster?', is how he described himself in his collection of poems, *Great Fear and the Moon*.

He was born in 1896 to a Hassidic family, raised in Lvov and, at 20, published his first poems in Yiddish and Hebrew. In the Great War, he was drafted into the Austrian Army, and deserted two years later. Upon returning to Lvov, he was shattered by the pogroms of November 1918. He moved to Warsaw and then Berlin, before immigrating to Palestine in 1924. He was welcomed by the Socialist movement, adopted as their poet, but in 1929, following the Arab riots and the massacre of numerous Jews, he aligned himself with the right-wing Revisionist movement, becoming one of its extremist activists, deploring the self-restrained policy towards the Arabs and the British.

Greenberg returned to Poland to work for the Revisionist movement, and was acutely apprehensive of the imminent catastrophe hovering over the heads of Jews, and he constantly urged them to save themselves. 'His parents, his six sisters, their husbands and their children begged to come to Palestine, but he was unable to take this personal commitment upon himself', says his wife Aliza:

> His character was such that he could not dedicate himself to anything that was not at the centre of his spiritual world. He had strong prophetic powers and on one occasion a friend came to his room in a Warsaw hotel, found the shutters closed and Uri lying on a wet sheet. 'What happened?', he asked. Uri replied, 'I cried all night. I know that they will all be destroyed'.

He wrote in 'Great Fear and the Moon':

> How can I not tremble with the fear of death by night? I remember the earth, thick and black, and the worms creeping on the dead / and the corpse lying warm and naked which will yet be mine. But now – the bed is made – there is a smell of women in the room.

Greenberg escaped from Warsaw in September 1939, during the first days of the War, using a press pass issued by *Der Moment*, a Yiddish Revisionist newspaper, which he edited and wrote for. 'He saves his skin, jumps over the dead, and lives/ an orphan of tortured martyrs who lie in the valley', as he later described his escape. His guilt at having failed to rescue his dear ones left him paralyzed. For the six years of the Second World War, he was in a state of shock, and did not publish a single poem.

> They were thrown into the pits with no memorial prayer / face and back bleeding and torn apart / just covered over with a hoe and sealed with jackboots / sprawling in dust – their loss is complete / they are no longer in the world … it is so quiet now! … and among those who lie hidden are my slaughtered parents / my sisters, their husbands and the tiny grandchildren – / dismembered vines!

These lines, from 'A Crown of Lament for the Whole People of Israel', are one of the first Uri-Zvi Greenberg published after the War. The following years, and the establishment of the State of Israel, were for him like the threshold of salvation.

> When I asked him, 'Why don't you dedicate your book *Streets of the River* to your mother and father?', he was appalled: 'How can I dedicate a book to my own family when not only they but the whole Jewish People have been destroyed?!' Only when they had all perished, he decided to marry. He felt an obligation to replace the family that had been slaughtered.

Says Aliza. She divorced her husband, and she and Greenberg married in 1950, when Uri-Zvi was 54 and his bride, 24. One after the other, within six and a half years they had five children. Uri-Zvi gave each of them two names, careful not to omit any of the victims among his own family. He named his eldest son Hayim Eliezer, for his father and grandfather. His second child, Bat-Sheva Shlomzion, was named after his mother and one of his sisters. The next daughter, Rivka-Havatselet Lev-Tsion, was named after two other murdered sisters; and the third daughter, Yocheved-Rachel Bat-Tsion, after two more sisters. The youngest son, David-Yehonatan, was named after Aliza's father.

When he first came to Palestine in the early 1920s, he went up to Jerusalem, to Tur-Malka on the top of the Mount of Olives, overlooking the city and the desert. According to a legend, the olives that grew here were used to make the anointing oil for the Biblical Kings. Wishing to symbolize his new life, he adopted the name Tur Malka as a new Hebrew pen-name. He used it only once, and years later gave it to his wife, herself a poet, to use.

Uri-Zvi Greenberg believed in the Divine Election of Israel as the Chosen People, and in the Covenant between God and Abraham, later renewed on Mount Sinai, as the basis of Jewish existence. For him, every deed in the present and the future must be derived from the glorious past, and his aim was to re-build the Kingdom of Israel as it was under golden days of King David. Believing that the ultimate role of poetry was to express the Messianic vision, he thought any Hebrew creative artist of this generation was compelled to harness writing for the benefit of the Jewish People.

Life with Uri-Zvi Greenberg was fraught with loneliness, and his wife and children, too, carried the burden of living with a hard, uncompromising man, who stood up for his principles and bore the brunt of ostracism and boycott which he encountered because of his nationalist views.

'Uri was very sensitive to anything fake, or to lack of talent', says Aliza Tur-Malka-Greenberg:

> He was very particular with not only what he wrote, but where it was to be published. Only if the editor took great pains with the proofreading and did not change a coma, would Uri continue to send him poems. If he published in a newspaper, which subsequently printed an article critical of the State of Israel, he would be deeply upset and never publish anything there again. I knew that I mustn't commit the great sin of compelling him to write for the sake of earning a living. So we lived with great frugality.

He could not be bought at any price. When an admirer wanted to award him a grant, Greenberg wrote an offensive letter, indignant, how could anyone dare offer him such a thing, 'He would walk from Tel Aviv to Jerusalem with gaping soles held together by a string', recounts Aliza Tur-Malka-Greenberg:

> Once, a posh car, with Ben-Gurion sitting inside, stopped to offer him a lift. Ben-Gurion invited him in, and he refused. 'How much do you want?', asked Ben-Gurion, and Uri replied: 'All the money that you have is not enough to buy me'. Ben-Gurion told him: 'We may have lost you, but you have also lost us'. When Zalman Aranne was Minister of Education, he too wanted to support us, but was afraid even to make an offer. Uri preferred poverty to servitude.

In the Greenberg Archives at the National Library in Jerusalem, there is a check from 1964 for 2,000 Israeli pounds, made out to Uri-Zvi Greenberg, drawn on Ben-Gurrion's private account. It was equivalent to a year's salary. Greenberg never cashed it.

With five young children, Aliza could not go out to work. 'But it wasn't the children so much as him. He was harder for me than 50 children', she almost whispers:

> Read Tolstoy's biography and you'll understand what it was like. If I say it wasn't easy, that's putting it mildly. I was caught

between the hammer and the anvil. Keeping the children from making a noise and disturbing him. Such a man was concentrated on his writing to the extreme; any interruption was a catastrophe for him. I'd rather not say what happened when a child interrupted him. He was a man of fury; he poured forth blazing wrath in his writing as well as in life. He was temperamental, tense and highly irritable.

When he was young he smoked 60 cigarettes a day, later switching to a pipe. He would write for hours and then sometimes go for a walk. He loved to see people; look at the crows on the telephone lines; gaze at the Yarkon River. He watched over himself very carefully, avoiding all kinds of dangers, since he felt that no one could carry out his mission, and seek the fount of prophecy. Despite his asceticism, he loved to be photographed. Whenever a photographer came to the house, Uri-Zvi Greenberg would theatrically pose for him. He had a regular column in the Ramat Gan local newspaper; a platform for his views which he took very seriously. 'He could express his political opinions there, his faith in the Kingdom of Israel, without any reservations. Then he would cut out the page and send it to the politicians to read', says his wife.

When he wrote, there would be scraps of paper scattered all over the house. He scribbled poems on bits of paper, used envelopes, the bindings of books. He allowed nothing to be touched. If his wife moved his books from their place, he would explode:

> I never peeped at any poem on his table, and read it only when it was printed in the newspaper. He was not a man to ask you for your opinion, always followed his mood; no one had any control over him. Uri would work a lot on a poem, writing many drafts. He told me he is willing to polish a poem endlessly, even just for a one sharp-eyed unknown reader.

Unlike writing, which came to him with much effort, he could draw with ease – humorous, frivolous sketches, which didn't seem to have emerged from the same tormented brain; the three books of poems that his wife wrote are illustrated by his sketches, 'In order to write words he had to feel them to their very depths. He once took a piece of the children's Plasticine and fashioned a bust of Hitler. It was frightening'. He was very musical, loved Bach, which reminded him of the music in the Temple, and enjoyed ancient Greek liturgical music. His poem 'Great Fear and the Moon' had a musical rhythm that he was not aware of while writing. Every morning he would pray directly to God, observing the Shabbat and the religious festivals with all their rituals. It didn't stop him saying that Jesus Christ 'lived a Jew and died a Jew, he was a Jew'.

*–'Have you seen him happy?'*
'He didn't know how to rejoice, even his happiness when the children were born, was mixed with great pain. How could he celebrate, when his family and the whole of the Jewish People had been destroyed? Sometimes he would ask me to sing the children lullabies that my father used to sing to me, liturgical hymns from the prayer book. He rarely laughed, there was a time when he cried a lot; he was a man who had seen so many disasters, whose life was full of the dead. He and his family were up against the wall in a pogrom in Lvov and they escaped by a last-minute miracle. Ten years later, in the Arab riots in Palestine, he had seen mutilated bodies of Jews, and slipped through the Jaffa Gate in Jerusalem to encounter Arabs dancing with long sharp knives, shouting "slaughter all Jews!" After the Holocaust, he envisioned the dreadful deaths that had befallen his sisters. This was not a literary metaphor, for him life came before literature. He would lie in bed at night, his eyes open. I would ask him, "Why are your eyes open? Do you want to see horrors in the dark?"'

Uri-Zvi Greenberg built a house in Ramat Gan, a small, modest home where his widow lives to this day. The furniture has not been changed for decades. His portrait hangs on the wall. A few drawings. No television set.

Not one of their five children took up writing. They seem still to be in awe of the talent and criticism of their parents. 'I have never nagged them to read their father. I believed it would have to come naturally', says Aliza. 'It's a huge, depressing body of work, I too find it painful to contemplate the burden of his suffering'.

Aliza Tur-Malka-Greenberg remembers in detail anyone who was ever kind to her husband, 'The truly great: Brenner, Bialik, Natan Alterman – they admired him, despite their political differences of opinion'. She can precisely quote hostile reviews years after they were published, nursing a grievance and taking vengeance for unpleasant remarks, never forgiving a man who called her husband 'murderer'. She enumerates all the injustices practiced against him:

> He was used to being persecuted and boycotted. When all kinds
> of offenses were committed against him, no one fought his wars
> for him. He never sought honours or status. When personally
> wounded, he never reacted unless it was an infringement upon
> the honour of Jerusalem.

For years he fumed that the Israeli postal service used the name
'Jerusalem' in its English postmark, and not the Hebrew pronunci-
ation 'Yerushalayim'. His wife continued the struggle after his death
and succeeded in bringing about the change. She is angry that Uri-
Zvi Greenberg's poetry is not compulsory reading in high school.
'It's evidence of his power, the boycott and the censorship continue,
they are afraid of the influence he might have. Never mind, the
truth of his poetry will win out and be recognized one day'.

In 1948, Uri-Zvi Greenberg was elected to the First Knesset,
where he held the honourable place of Number Two on the Herut
list (the Revisionist party), after Menachem Begin, the leader of the
right-wing underground group Irgun Tsvai Leumi. The parliamentary records reveal that he was a conscientious member, who fought
for the status of Jerusalem, and a fierce opponent of taking repara-
tion money from Germany and the normalization of ties between
the two nations. He quit parliament after one term, a prophet of
wrath, later crowned with literary prizes, but remained a contro-
versial public figure. He was awarded the Israel Prize for literature
in 1957, but never wanted to be a candidate for the Nobel Prize.
'He refused to be liked by the Gentiles', says his wife.

When he was a Member of the Knesset, he often met Prime
Minister Ben-Gurion, who listened to him with great respect. 'Ben-
Gurion told him, "You have a carnal love for the Land of Israel" and
Uri liked the expression and saw it as a compliment', says Aliza
Greenberg:

> People wanted to hear his views, for he had a profound intellec-
> tual grasp. He wrote, 'If we retreat one metre from the Suez
> Canal, blood will stain Mount Hermon'. He liked to meet army
> generals like Moshe Dayan and Arik Sharon. Once Dayan said
> to him, 'What do we need this nuisance of Sinai and Sharm a-
> Shekh for?' Uri replied, 'If you give up Sinai you will have to
> argue over Jerusalem'. Minister Zalman Aranne came to our

house and consulted him how to increase Jewish consciousness in Israeli youth. Uri took him to the window and said, 'You, in the Labour Party, have tried to enter the house through the window, but you have to educate the nation to come in through the door, and return to our sources, the Jewish tradition, everything we have cut ourselves off from'.

Although Greenberg loved Jerusalem with all his heart, he never lived there. He would travel to Jerusalem and then return home. He could not bear to look at the ruins of the Temple Mount. He and Agnon would wander for hours about the city like a pair of sleepwalkers, drawn by an immense attraction. 'The Valley of Jezreel is the tefillin for the arm and Jerusalem is the tefillin for the head', wrote Greenberg.

After the Six Day War, Greenberg took his wife and rushed to pray on Temple Mount:

> There was a Moslem clergyman standing there waving his hands for us to go away, and an IDF [Israeli Defence Force] officer, who said to me, 'Tell your husband this is a holy place'. I kept silent. The officer went up to Uri and told him, 'You should know that this is a holy Moslem place'. Uri was startled. Then he turned to me and said, 'Aliza, as from this moment I am leaving the Temple Mount for ever'. He bent down, took a handful of earth, wrapped it in a handkerchief and went to the Western Wall to finish his prayer.

He rejoiced in 1977, when the Likud party won the elections, but was quickly disappointed when Prime Minister Menachem Begin gave up Sinai in exchange for peace with Egypt. General Yosef Geva remembered that after the signing of the Camp David agreements he was walking through the Jewish Quarter of Old Jerusalem with Uri-Zvi, who said to him, 'We need a few people who can sort things out and save us from this disaster called Begin'. Then he asked Geva to murder Begin. 'Why me?' the general asked. 'Because they'll never suspect you', said Uri-Zvi Greenberg. His wife believes that, 'It was just a way of speaking'.

Uri-Zvi Greenberg stopped writing in 1978. His last years were spent in a mist. 'When he was institutionalized and already distracted and suffering from loss of memory', says Aliza:

I read him a poem I had published and he said: 'That's nice. You have entered the soul of the landscape.' It surprised me that poetry was still a part of him, even though he had forgotten much of his life.

He died at the age of 84, on the eve of Independence Day, 1981. His followers considered it symbolic that he passed away surrounded by blue and white flags.

## TRANSLATED INTO ENGLISH

U.-Z. Greenberg, *Jerusalem* [trans. C.A. Cowen] (New York: Blackstone Publishers, 1939).

# CHAPTER THREE

# Natan Alterman
## (1910–70)

# Lava of Love and Politics

Natan Alterman never kept a diary. In the few letters that he wrote he uncovered little about himself; too much of an introvert to reveal his heart even to the few friends he had. Only in his poems did he speak frankly, they were the couch on which he lay, divulging his inner conflicts.

He was born in Warsaw in 1910, to a dominant, overpowering father, an educationalist who founded the first Hebrew nursery and seminar for nursery teachers. A sociable man full of zest, initiative and a sense of humour, Yitzhak Alterman was the opposite of his wife Bella, a cold, introverted dentist absorbed in her work and in her own affairs. She maintained a symbiotic relationship with her mother who lived with them, and was emotionally tied to her husband's sister; an attachment so powerful that Professor Dan Miron, Alterman's biographer, suspects that Bella Alterman, 'was probably a woman whose deepest emotional ties were with other women'.

'Mother, do not desert the Shrine of the Home / do not speak out at women's conventions', wrote the 21-year-old Natan Alterman in a poem deeply influenced by Richard Wagner: an anti-feminist outcry; a desperate appeal to his mother, a manifestation of a modern woman striving for liberation from her domestic role. He begged her to remain true to her natural, biological destiny, but at the same time, he feared the intoxicating attraction of woman's sexuality. This conflict was never resolved and coloured both his life and his poetry. Later in life, poems of praise of the Wife and Mother turned into poems of murderous jealousy: 'Let my raging envy gush forth/ and burn your home upon you'. In his love poetry, the sexes always battled, the relationships violent and vulnerable.

*Butterfly from the Larva* is the title of Miron's first volume of Alterman's biography, published in Hebrew in 2001. 'The image fits Alterman perfectly: he had a sombre, constricted, depressing child-hood, like a larva, but managed to break through and rise into a brilliant, colourful butterfly'.

Scores of writers moved in and out of his parents' home, some stayed as houseguests for extended periods and they all lavished attention on the boy, who suffered from the incessant over-stimula-tion of people entirely concerned with their own affairs. They were amused by his childish company, but not concerned for his normal, undisturbed development. From a young age he reacted to this over-attention by turning in on himself. Among the visitors to the house were Bialik, Genessin, and Y. L. Peretz. This was the beginning of a compulsive but ambivalent relationship with literature and its heroes: Alterman's admiration for the world of the word was coupled with a need for an ordinary life. Young Natan imitated the poetry of Bialik, whom his father admired, and plagiarized lines from well-known poets.

At the Gymnasia Hertzliya, the leading high school in Tel Aviv, where he began studying immediately after the family immigrated to Palestine in 1925, he was so self-effacing, that even after he became famous as the greatest poet of his generation, his classmates remembered only the pale, nondescript youth who did not excel at anything. Natan's early poems were conventional and bad, the verse of a 'good boy' who wishes to please his parents. His teacher, Baruch Ben-Yehuda, later principal of the school, has affirmed that:

> ... if I had been told then, when I was his teacher, that this boy would become a poet, a moulder of public opinion, a man of public conscience, I would not have believed it ... Natan was taciturn, his reticence was affected also by the difficulty he had in speaking, he stammered a lot more than in later years ... I have preserved records of all the classes that I taught, but I have found nothing whatsoever about Natan.

Alterman's only friend at school was the most intimidated boy in the class, to whom he extended his patronage, rather like a plain girl who chooses a girl plainer than herself for a companion. Later, at the height of his popularity, when he was intimate with heads of state and army generals – who regarded him as the nation's conscience and sought his advice – he became a one-man 'welfare office'. He pulled strings among his powerful friends for hundreds of people, while he himself led an austere life. In the 1950s, Alterman's friends offered him a private house in an affluent suburb for high-ranking army officers, which had been built near Tel Aviv. 'They said that his contribution to the State was no less than any army general's', says Professor Miron:

> Alterman argued, 'And what if I would want to write about you?' The officials said, 'No strings attached, you are free to write whatever you like'. 'But if I want to praise you, people will think that I am biased'. And he turned the offer down.

When he finished high school, his extreme shyness made him unsuitable to what was considered the height of aspiration: to study law in England and strive to be a lawyer in the Jewish community of Palestine. His father, who feared that Natan would be forced to rely on a precarious income from journalism and poetry, pushed him towards the next best alternative, to study medicine in France, arguing that Natan's stammer would not be too much of an impediment, 'since a doctor doesn't have to talk much'. Eventually, young Alterman was enrolled in agronomy, an occupation for which he had no inclination.

At the outset of his French stay, he was depressed and homesick for the small-town intimacy of Tel Aviv, but he very soon began to open up and go forth on a journey of self-discovery. Paris bowled him over: the bridges, the streetlights, and the people – everything attracted him. Twenty-year-old Natan roamed the streets, and could not keep his eyes off the grand statues in the Jardins des Tuileries, and the fountains bubbling like champagne. He imagined himself as a vagrant, at large in the seductive, fevered concrete jungle. Paris was the first occasion ever that he was away from the family home; it was a place attractive and repellent, castrating with its suffocating love:

> As he sat in the cafés and bars, listening to the witty songs of the *chansonnières*, undressing the waitresses and the whores with his

gaze and dreaming of passionate embraces in their arms, Alterman was obliged to 'murder' the 'good boy' within him.

Says Professor Dan Miron, from Tel Aviv University. 'In his later poetry, he developed the idea of "the double", the twin, the innocent Abel who is killed or abandoned in his sickness by Cain'.

France made Alterman's poetry erotic, revealing sexuality, fear of castration, violence and sadomasochistic tendencies. In 'A Woman's Fragrance', a poem that he never published, he compared a stunning Parisian whore he had met – fascinating but deceitful – to his father, the most significant figure in his life: 'Like Father you spread fragrance / and like him nothing more! You are like father ... and like him / the flesh of your hands a harlot's pay myrrh'.

Alterman returned to Tel Aviv in 1933, a certified agronomist, but his father soon realized that the money he invested in his son's education, was a waste: it had not swayed him from his true vocation of poetry. Alterman's first poems had already been published in 1931, and received high acclaim. It is not accidental that he chose to publish them in the magazine *Ktuvim*, edited by Avraham Shlonsky, a harsh critic of Bialik. His father being a great admirer of the national poet, Natan was flaunting his independence and opting for a substitute father figure. 'Shlonsky suited him, because he advocated poetics of rationality, and Alterman looked for ways to restrain the lava burning inside him', says Professor Dan Miron. 'In later years, when Natan Zach and his generation criticized Alterman for his precise, symmetric verse, he excused himself that these measures guard one from getting loose'.

In 1935, after two failed love affairs, Alterman married actress Rachel Marcus. He knew from the start that their love life was doomed to be a failure, but he expected little from marriage anyhow. From an early age, he sensed that any permanent relationship between a man and a woman would end in pain and injury. Love between his parents had long since faded, and his father had the reputation of a libertine, an adulterer, lacking control over his instincts. He was frequently absent from home, and stories were rampant about his liaisons with young school and nursery teachers. It is unclear what exactly Natan knew, but a poisonous, irksome kernel seeped into his consciousness and manifested itself in a tendency to depression and a lack of *joie de vivre*. His own love life would become complicated, estranged, split down the middle between his legal wife, and his mistress, Tsila Binder, whom he met four years after his marriage. Binder, ten years younger than him, was not separated from him even by his death, over 30 years later.

– *'Why didn't he divorce his wife and marry his mistress?'*
'I doubt whether he loved Tsila as well', says Professor Miron, 'He was a narcissist, loved to be loved and admired. Clearly it was all derived from low self-esteem. If he had inner strength, he would have had no need for incessant external reinforcements. He had very little talent for matrimony, rather, he had an "anti-talent" for it. I remember his home. There were three rooms in a row, Rachel's was on the left, and on the far right was Alterman's monk-like cell with a schoolboy's desk and a bookcase. The middle room was always empty, with just a folding table: a graphic representation of the total separation that existed between husband and wife. The extramarital affair provided him protection from being too exposed, too intimate with one woman. The right hand held off the left hand. His wife was a wonderfully nice person, a fine comic actress, and full of *élan vital*. She built a world of her own, unlike the mistress, who remained enslaved to him throughout her life. The mistress' love for him was obsessive and intense, and involved self-effacement. He dictated the terms of their affair, and she lived by them'.

The real victim of the threesome was Tirza, the beloved, bright, only child of the Altermans, born January 1941. She was a mixture of the symbolic contradictions of her mother, who was born on the day of the Purim carnival, and father, born on the fast of Tish'a Be'av', which commemorates the destruction of the Temple. While Rachel came to terms with her husband's infidelity, the daughter adopted the stance of the betrayed wife. 'To grow up in such an atmosphere of rift, especially for someone like Tirza, who was not particularly strong and healthy, was an emotional reality not easy to cope with', says Dan Miron.
     At 23, Tirza published her first collection of poetry, only after the approval of her scrutinizing father. She never rebelled against his poetic influence, and when challenged that her imagery was similar to his, she said, laughingly, 'The whole country copies from him, why can't I?' Her only transgression was to choose a different surname, 'Atar', which is a shortening of 'Alterman', and also means 'Location' in Hebrew.
     Alterman was many-sided: a prolific poet and a popular song-writer, a playwright, and a distinguished translator of Shakespeare,

Molière and Racine. His daughter followed in his footsteps, and was an actress, poet and translator. She met her husband on the stage, appearing in a play that her father had translated, and the young couple flew to New York to study at an actors' studio. A year later, Natan Alterman flew hastily to tend to his daughter following her nervous breakdown. After two months, they returned to Israel, and Tirza was back on stage and writing poetry that revealed an enormous fear of madness, loss of control, and death. 'Guard your soul, guard your life', pleaded the alarmed Alterman in one of his most famous poems, and she answered in lines of her own; 'I'm cautious of falling objects, of fire, of wind, of poems'.

Alterman had his regular table at the bohemian Café Kassit, always surrounded by fellow poets and groupies. More than an imitation of the Paris Left-Bank cafés, those of Tel Aviv resembled the Hassidic tradition of the 'Tisch', the long dinner table of the rabbi, surrounded by his followers, gulping down every word of his. Tsila forever at his table, he was always the leader of the band; and to encourage his admirers to drink, he paraphrased Charles Baudelaire:

> If you do not wish to feel the burden of time, leaning over your shoulders and grinding you to dust – always be drunk, endlessly. Be drunk with what? With wine, poetry, morals, as you wish. But always be drunk.

Physically, Natan Alterman was his mother's son. Like her, he had a high forehead, an aquiline nose, thin lips and a receding chin. But, when drunk, his face transformed into the crude, almost licentious expression of his father, who was extremely fond of alcohol. But while the father could hold his liqueur, Natan very quickly lost control and became cruel, brutish, violent, offensive and quite intolerable, even to his friends. 'I have seen him in such a state more than once. He used alcohol to shed his inhibitions and inner restraints', says Professor Dan Miron.

In 1938, Alterman published his first mature poetry collection, *Outdoor Stars*, and his new voice was instantly recognised. For the first time in Modern Hebrew literature, personal and intimate love took centre stage, free of nationalistic calling and historical burden. French and Russian Symbolist poets inspired Alterman, who was a master of the lyrical, meditative poetry. But the call of the times, the horrors of the Second World War, and the struggle for independence, encouraged him to discard lyrical poetry and to switch to political writing. In 1943 he began writing *The Seventh Column*, which was a weekly column of political verse in the daily newspaper *Davar*. For 24 years, until 1967, he documented and commented on major milestones in the making of Israel. While Bialik was often blunt and critical towards the shortcomings of the Jewish people, Alterman was a national poet of a different sort, a creator of communal consensus, a sensitive barometer and compass of the country's mood. 'We are the silver platter / upon which the Jewish State was served to you', he wrote in 'The Silver Platter', published in *Davar* in December 1947. It was shortly after the United Nations' decision to partition Palestine into Arab and Jewish states, and has since become a symbol of the high blood-price of independent existence.

Alterman was an ardent supporter of Ben-Gurion, who was a father figure to him, but, like a rebellious son, refused to be the court bard. He departed from the Prime Minister on two major issues: objecting to normalization of ties with Germany, and condemning the over-use of power by the Israeli Defence Forces towards Israeli Arabs. An avid reader of the poet, Ben-Gurion was aware of his public influence, and did not criticise him openly. In November 1948, Alterman's column portrayed a young soldier riding on his Jeep through the streets of an occupied town, gratuitously shooting an old Arab; Ben-Gurion had the poem printed and distributed to all army units.

In 1957, after 14 years of lyrical silence, Alterman published the much-awaited *Dove City*. Although the book won him the prestigious Bialik Prize for Literature, it received mixed reviews: instead of intimate poetry, Alterman had produced an epos of the birth of a new Jewish kingdom.

The Six Day War of 1967, and the capture of Jerusalem and the West Bank, transformed Alterman. He broke away from a lifetime in the service of the Labour party, and became a fierce supporter and a major spokesman of the right-wing Eretz Israel Hashlema [The Greater Land of Israel].

For decades, Natan Alterman lived with the trauma of his father's death. In 1935, Yitzhak Alterman was diagnosed with cancer of the throat, and his son went to Paris with him for the operation. But metastasis had taken place; there was nothing to be done. 'For the father shall not die, he is eternally a father / he shall go down living to hell', wrote Alterman in his poem 'The End of the Father'.

His father was 58 at his death, and Alterman convinced himself that he too would not live much longer. He always neglected his health, with his heavy drinking and destructive way of life. Suffering severe stomach pains, he disregarded them out of fear; certain it was a malignant tumour. He refused to be examined and was tormented with pain for months. He was unaware that his only illness was peritonitis, and when finally was rushed to hospital for an operation in March 1970, he lapsed into a coma, due to a mishap under anaesthesia. Two weeks later he died, aged only 60.

His only daughter found it hard to continue without him. Married for the second time, with two small children, she longed for him in her poems. In September 1977, she fell from her bedroom window six floors down to her death.

## TRANSLATIONS INTO ENGLISH

Altermann, N., *Selected Poems* [trans. R. Friend] (Tel Aviv: Hakibutz Hameuchad Publishing House, 1978).
—— *Little Tel Aviv* [*Tel Aviv Haktana*; trans. Y. Tobin] (Tel Aviv: Hakibutz Hameuchad Publishing House, 1981).

# CHAPTER FOUR

# Leah Goldberg
## (1911–70)

# Cursed by Love

On the morning of the day before she lost her consciousness and became immersed into the sleep that she never awoke from, the 59-year-old Leah Goldberg opened her eyes suddenly, with a frightened stare and asked weakly, 'But mother! What would become of mother?'

'I could not tell her that we would look after her mother. It would have been an admittance that she was about to die', recalls her secretary and close friend, Yehudit Price. 'When the nurse signalled us to leave, I put my hand on the mother's shoulder and together we left the room. I hoped Leah saw us and believed that her mother was not left alone in the world'.

It was 15 January 1970. Twelve years later, at the age of 90, Tsila Goldberg died, and was buried next to her daughter under the pine trees at 'The University Plot', in the Jerusalem Har Hamenuchot Cemetery. At her request, her tombstone was engraved with the words: 'The mother of poet Leah Goldberg'.

This was the single, most stable and meaningful relationship in the lives of the two: Tsila Goldberg, who divorced a mentally ill husband, and her only daughter Leah, who never got married. Throughout their entire lives, the mother and daughter had lived together in one apartment, a deep, symbiotic and extremely close alliance.

Leah Goldberg was born in May 1911, in the town of Koenigsberg (now Kalinigrad), and grew up in Kovno (now Kaunas), Lithuania. With the outbreak of the Great War, her family fled into the depths of Russia. Once, her mother recalled, when they were both sailing on the Volga river, she heard the infant Leah reciting a few lines she had made up, in fluent Russian, 'Oh birds, birds, where are you flying to?' The mother was frightened of the child's hypersensitivity and precocious talent.

In exile, Leah's only brother, Emmanuel, was born, but died of meningitis before his first birthday. The deceased brother accompanied Goldberg throughout her life, and would emerge in her writing in different forms: Emmanuel – that's how she named her deserting lover in 'Letters from a Fictional Journey'.

When they returned by train from Russia at the end of the War, her greatest tragedy occurred, as her father, a renowned economist, the founder of the Lithuanian social security services, was arrested at the border: the yellow-reddish shoes that he was wearing were a sure sign (in the soldiers' eyes) that he was a member of the Communist Party. Her mother went to plead with them for his release, and Leah was left alone in the barren, freezing field, to guard the family luggage. 'Tremendous fear crept over me, but I did not cry. I was not afraid of evil beasts. I was eight years old, and already knew that Evilness comes from man, not beast', she wrote in her memoirs.

For ten days in a row the soldiers would take the father out of his prison cell, tie his eyes and face him to the wall, in front of a firing squad. With great effort, Tsila Goldberg managed to release her husband, and they returned to Kovno. But the ordeal had wrecked his nerves and triggered a hereditary mental illness. From a gentle, educated man, who nourished his daughter, the father was transformed into an unruly, wild person, who believed he was God or the Messiah. At first he was kept at home, but when his behaviour became too risky, he was moved to a mental institution. Leah used to visit him there – cherishing his rare momentary lapses into sanity – to stroll and converse with him, as they used to.

She recalled the pain in her autobiographical novel, *And He the Light*, where the father of her heroine, Nora, visits her during school break:

> ... his eyes, distant and harsh, wandering across the yard, over the children running wild. Fear shivers through Nora's body. She

knows what the meaning of the eyes is ... 'Father', pleads Nora, 'Do not walk with me, they laugh'. 'The children will understand, Nora, I will tell them, tell them the truth', says the father. He raises his walking stick. A great blaze sparkles in his eyes. 'Father!' she calls, desperately. Suddenly, first sounds of laughter are heard, calls of 'Lunatic!' 'This is the father of Nora Krigger, he is a lunatic!'

Accidentally discovering in adolescence that her father's brother also suffered from the mental illness that plagued the entire family, Leah Goldberg was shaken: 'I very much fear that my father has passed his illness to me as well', wrote the 15-year-old in her diary:

> If this is the case, I must not deceive myself. The mentally ill must not think of their private happiness. They must not marry, for they destroy the lives of their spouses. They must not give birth to children, for they pass their illness to them and make them miserable as well.

Was it just a coincidence that Leah Goldberg never married or had children, or perhaps it was a conscious wish on her part, to prevent others from the fate of her mother and of herself as a child? The poet, Tuvia Ribner, a close friend for dozens of years, and the executor of her literary estate said:

> The memory of the father and her fear accompanied Leah to adulthood. This is the reason, I believe, that she chose the stricter poetic forms, such as a sonnet, which has 14 lines, meticulous rhyming scheme and fixed rhythm, and avoided loose rhythms. Her poetics emerge from a strong need for self-control, every single one of her poems having a rational basis, meant to guard the poem and herself.

The Hebrew school in Kovno was a nightmare for Leah, recalls Mina Landau, her classmate:

> The childhood years of exile imprinted the Russian language in her, and she dreamt, spoke and read in Russian. She had no knowledge of Hebrew and could not speak or understand a single word of Yiddish. The children conspired against her and beat her up, claiming that she refused to speak Yiddish out of haughtiness. Since she was an introvert, she was an easy prey.

In her diary, began at age ten and continued throughout life, she wrote:

> And what if all of a sudden all my dreams were to come true, would I have been happy? Of course not, I would have found myself other troubles, and if there were no realistic ones, I would have made them up. It is my nature not to be content. A happy person could only be he who carries happiness within himself; he who seeks happiness from the outside, will never find it. I belong to the latter kind.

Still, she was attracted to romance, and used to cut out magazine pictures of women and men, arrange them in pairs, and contrive stories of love and adultery.

'To become a writer, on this I trust my future and my life', she decided at 15. 'This is my single goal, and if I do not reach it, then I do not care what life makes of me'. Her father's illness impoverished and split the parents and, after their divorce, Leah became a nanny and a private tutor to finance her studies in linguistics at the University of Berlin. At only 22, she was awarded a PhD at the University of Bonn for her brilliant thesis on Semitic languages. However, her academic career was not in linguistics but in Comparative Literature, and she used her ear for languages to study Norwegian in order to translate *Per Gynt* into Hebrew; and Italian, for Petrarch's sonnets.

Her first Hebrew poems were published in 1932 and, thanks to a precious entry visa sent to her by the prominent poet, Avraham Shlonsky, Goldberg was able to immigrate to Palestine in the spring of 1935, to be joined by her mother a year later. Since entry visas were extremely limited, the Jewish Agency deceived the British Mandate Authorities and set up an 'arranged marriage' for the owner of the visa, thus gaining entry for two instead of one. Goldberg and her supposed 'spouse' – the writer Shimon Gantz – separated as soon as they touched land, but when her friends leafed through her identity card after her death, they were amazed to see that under 'family status', she declared herself 'divorced'. In their eyes, this was a proof of honesty: even though the marriage was only a trick, she refused to be falsely counted a spinster. Or, perhaps, it was a manifestation of her secret wish to be a lawful wedded wife?

Already, at 24, she was an esteemed, promising poet, and the established Shlonsky surprised her with a present on her arrival: a collection of her verse, titled *Rings of Smoke*, which he had compiled and published. But the roses of welcome turned into thorns, as she was deeply disappointed that the book was strewn with misprints. Goldberg lived the bohemian life, debating for days on end with her poet friends in the Tel Aviv cafés. To finance their poetry, she and other members of the *Yachdav* [Together] – a modernist literary group comprising Avraham Shlonsky, Natan Alterman, Yaakov Horowitz, Israel Zemora – supported themselves by writing commercials. The one that she did for Shemen Cooking Oil was a huge marketing success.

Goldberg lived with her mother, rushing between her jobs as schoolteacher, journalist, editor of children's books, translator, and literary and theatre critic. However, she gave this up when she realized that being a critic cost her the few friends she had. Always fond of children, she was the co-editor of the highly acclaimed children's and youths' weekly, *Davar Liladim*, and wrote rhymes accompanied by the drawings of her close friend, Aryeh Navon. A gifted painter in her childhood, she abandoned the colours and the brush in favour of the word. She only returned to painting and collages when she was in her fifties. 'The picture is more tangible than the word', she now said. In middle age, like an adolescent, she drew beautiful princesses with flowing long hair; continuing to feel the detachment and haughtiness of the princess buried inside her.

'At times of lack of inspiration in writing, she turned to painting. She often made sketches of the literary protagonists who furnished her life, as she visualized them in her imagination', remembers her friend, the poet T. Carmi.

Generations of Israeli girls and women still grow up on Goldberg's agonizing love poems, which reflect her miserable, impossible and unilateral relations with men, many of whom were as old as her father. At 14 and a half, Leah fell in love with her 35-year-old history teacher, and at 16 she pined for three years, yearning for her literature teacher. In her diary she wrote, 'I cannot love a man who loves me in return'.

She was 28 when she met the love of her life. 'Our bodies united with no animosity or fear', she wishfully wrote in 'A Love Poem from an Ancient Book', about poet Avraham Ben-Yitzhak (Dr Avraham Sone) who ruled her heart for 11 years, until his death in 1950. An introverted, solemn, ascetic, fascinating man, Dr Avraham

Ben-Yitzhak Sone, who was twice her age, held a senior office at the Jewish Agency. He was a squeamish man, who published only 11 poems in his entire life, all considered exceptional. His influence on Goldberg was immense. 'S. is poison in my bones', she wrote in her diary on 4 January 1944. 'I know that my intellect does not reach the wisdom of S., but I need a man like him at my side. A man one slightly fears and respects (a school-girl term –"admire")'.

There was no other woman in his life, and yet a relationship never materialized, for reasons unknown. 'She suffered from emotional deficiency, that made her incapable of establishing an intimate relationship with a man', says the psychologist Professor Amiya Leiblich, who wrote a biography of Goldberg, To Leah.

> It may have resulted from an inner ugliness, which was imbued in her. People who do not believe they deserve love, fulfil it by unconsciously choosing partners who will not love them in return. She had a permanent guilt towards all the men she was in love with, as well as an inferiority complex. Even in poetry, where her value and superiority were unmistakable, she always thought she was lacking, and not as good as Ben-Yitzhak. As a feminist, I am indignant that a poet as great as Goldberg, erased herself, not just as a woman, but as an artist.

After a long separation, with Sone already very ill, they met a few times in the last year of his life:

> Sone died on my birthday. Since then, nothing else matters. I only feel the burden, the fear of life itself, helplessness and an internal emptiness. After his death I find it hard to be interested in other people, everything is faulty and cannot be restored. I do not write, for most of this year I have not written a thing. I am very worn out.

Two years later, she found within herself the strength to document their relationship in the book, A Meeting with a Poet. The dead Sone kept haunting her dreams, taking her hand in his, going on walks:

> His hand was warm and mine was cold. I told him, 'How warm your hand is', and he laughed and took my hand in his second hand as well. And I loved him dearly. With this I woke up almost at the first light of dawn.

She was always guarding her secrets behind walls, and her love poems were covered under seven veils of mystery; among her most beautiful is the sonnet sequence, 'The Love of Theresa De-Mon', which is about a fictitious sixteenth-century noble Italian lady who desperately falls for her children's tutor and thus breaks all taboos of age, family and class. 'This violent curse which plagued me / that, which the innocent call love', is one of the most well-known lines. The young tutor does not reciprocate, never imagining that he haunts the dreams of that grey-haired lady, the mother of his pupils. When he leaves, Theresa De-Mon retires into a convent.

Only in the 1990s, decades after Goldberg's death, when her diaries – kept in the Gnazim Writers' Archives in Tel Aviv – were finally made available to researchers, was the identity of the man who triggered 'Theresa De-Mon' unveiled. He was a Swiss lecturer in literature, who came for a sabbatical at the Hebrew University in the early 1950s. Brought up on Western culture and art, no wonder that Dr Goldberg, a lecturer in Comparative Literature, found in the young Swiss a magic that she was missing in her mundane existence.

'He was very young looking, handsome, a foreigner ... but not at all similar to the image I contrived, because of my need to love somebody', Leah Goldberg wrote in her diary:

> I know perfectly well that this boy cannot see in me anything but an older and more experienced friend, someone to talk to sometimes, an elderly lady that must not see herself as worthy of love. It does not insult me one bit. Maybe I'm quite happy by this falling in love.

After three and a half years in Jerusalem he returned to the University of Lausanne not suspecting that he had been loved by his colleague, 'He awoke me to life, and did something for the Hebrew literature', Goldberg wrote to herself.

'It's amazing that Leah Goldberg described herself in the poems and in her diary, as a middle-aged woman, and him as a man who could almost be her son', says biographer Professor Leiblich:

> I checked the dates: she was 41 years old and he, 38, quite close to her age. But from an early stage, she felt herself old, heavy, too serious. She had a sense of guilt about all her loves, she perceived love as a nuisance, something to beware of.

Jerusalem, adorned with the memories of the past, appealed to her more than the 'white cardboard boxes', which she associated with Tel Aviv. She was a fascinating university lecturer, who loved to stand on the pedestal, her eternal cigarette in her hand, and read poetry in her deep, rough, unpleasant voice, that nevertheless drew crowds into over-stuffed auditoriums. It was considered a great privilege to attend the Tuesday evening seminars at her home. Although she became the Head of Comparative Literature Studies, she remained alien in the academic establishment. 'Being both an artist and a woman, the male colleagues belittled her academic achievements, and she had a hard struggle to be nominated as a professor', recalls Esther Tishbi, a friend.

Leah Goldberg expanded the spectrum of lyricism, her poems speaking of a search for love, contact and attention, and she inspired hordes of young poets, mostly women. But she became an easy target for the new rebellious generation of poets and critics, who feared to attack the male figureheads like Shlonsky and Alterman. She complained to Tuvia Ribner, 'What do they want from me, I was never at the centre of the stage. Why do they pick on me?'

The intense relationship with her mother dominated her life, and what began as an economic necessity, became second nature. Her mother was the fulcrum of her life, the practical force, the common sense, 'Mrs Goldberg gave up on her own self willingly and devoted herself to serve her daughter, who was the centre of her world. She truly liberated Leah from all the practical disturbances of daily life', says her friend Esther Tishbi. Leah Goldberg highly appreciated her mother's literary taste, showed her poems before publication, and was willing to alter a line if her mother disapproved.

She had a special rapport with children, although, in her book *Miracles and Wonders*, she introduced herself as 'Nobody's Aunt'. Her children's books are still constant bestsellers and favourite bedtime stories in Israel. Children used to write to her in their thousands; she kept their letters and replied to them all, on colourful stationery that she bought especially on her European tours. One can only wonder if the constant presence of the mother in the next room, even when the daughter slowly aged, had not stood as a barrier between Leah and the experiences of matrimony and motherhood. It was such a close symbiosis that on the day of Leah's funeral the friends were amazed to hear Mrs Goldberg say, 'It is a good thing that Leah died before I did. If I died first, she would not have lasted a single day'.

To a friend, who visited her on her birthday in May 1969, Goldberg complained about her health, but delayed her visit to the doctor, because of her mother's eye surgery. When she was finally examined, it was too late to operate on the cancerous tumour in her breast. She began painting frantically, and two months before her death drew a broken stringed instrument with three people standing around it as if it was an open grave. The cigarettes she had smoked her entire life took their revenge on her and, soon afterwards, cancer was also found in her lungs.

'Leah Goldberg felt herself kin with Dante, Kafka, Beethoven, who also had imaginary loves, which were the muses that ignited their great works', concludes Professor Amiya Leiblich:

> First and foremost, she was a poet, willing to let go of life for art's sake. The woman who experienced a miserable love life, succeeded in producing gentle love poems, and remains Israel's High Priestess of Love, who couples quote in moments of the most intense emotional harmony.


## TRANSLATED INTO ENGLISH

Goldberg, L., *On the Blossoming* [*Al Hapricha*; trans. M.B. Sivan] (New York: Garland Publishers, Inc., 1992).
—— *Selected Poems of Leah Goldberg* [trans. R. Friend] (London: Menard Press/San Francisco, CA: Panjandrum Books, 1976).
—— *Lady of the Castle* (a play) [*Ba'alat Haarmon*; trans. T. Carmi] (Tel Aviv: Institute of Translation of Hebrew Literature, 1974).

# CHAPTER FIVE

# S. Yizhar
## (1916– )

# No Stone is Worth Dying For

When the nine o'clock TV news screened pictures of two soldiers kicking six Palestinian labourers in their testicles, jumping onto their backs, and slapping and punching them in their faces for fun, I thought of the young officer Yizhar Smilansky. Fifty years had passed since that day in the summer of 1948, in the midst of Israel's War of Independence, when his unit encountered a 40-year-old Arab shepherd. Out of boredom, just because it was a hot, irritating day, they tied the man's hands and blindfolded his eyes and dragged him along, roaring with laughter every time he stumbled and fell to the ground. Then came the blows – direct, well aimed:

> Again and again, ever more easily and naturally, a kick would flash out. Cold-blooded kicks, delivered without anger, just more skilled. Have no pity. Hit him. They wouldn't have any pity on you. Arabs are used to blows ... 'I'll be the one to finish him of'. The bald-headed one took on the job, and impatiently flicked away his cigarette.

When the shepherd was loaded onto the truck, it was clear to Yizhar that they should stop halfway and look aside while the innocent victim ran off to his wife and children, hoping he would forgive them, maybe even forget:

You hide behind the foul-smelling, 'What can you do – an order is an order', except that this time there is an alternative, it's within your power. A great day. A day of revolt. A day when finally the choice is in your hands. The power to decide. To grant life to an oppressed man. Go for it. Follow your heart. Your love. Your truth. Set him free. Be a man. Set him free!

But no one spared Hassan Ahmed; and he was destined to a bullet in the head or, if he was lucky, merely to torture. Those who stood aside, like the young officer Yizhar, were powerless against the current, never forgetting it, having nowhere to hide the disgrace. Yizhar, who recorded the incident in 1949 in his story 'The Prisoner', was labelled a 'bleeding heart' and was heaped with abuse and threatening letters. Later, when he published his monumental novel, *Tziklag Days*, shaking the heroic myth of the War of Independence, there were objections to awarding him the Israel Prize on the grounds that he had 'spoken ill of the IDF and blackened the reputation of Israeli youth'. Nevertheless, literature won, and he got the prize in 1959.

– *'Do you consider your war stories to have been prophetic?'*
'It was not so much prophesy as a description of reality, things I had seen with my own eyes. I am shocked by what is happening now in the West Bank, but I am not surprised; it is the inevitable result of the encounter between conqueror and conquered. No man should be allowed absolute power over others. We all have evil drives, and when given authority over defenceless people each one of us feels that he has a quasi-legitimacy to vent aggression and fury and malice, the excuse always being that one is facing an enemy. It is plain sadism and spiritual perversion, which derive their justification from so-called security and national needs. The rules of the game must be changed, and the perpetrators punished. I would court-martial soldiers who abuse power, so it would be a lesson for all their comrades'.

Born in 1916 to a family of writers, into the bright orange of rural Palestine, his pioneer parents, Miriam and Ze'ev Smilansky named him after the 'glow' [*zohar*] of the sun. In using this as his pen-name, Yizhar (the mythological Sabra) ensured that he would always be addressed by his fresh, first name.

His rich literary prose is highly poetic, long rhythmic passages alternating with short ones, the long interior monologue being the hallmark of his style. *Preludes* begins with a description of the world from the point of view of a two year old whose father has taken him to the fields and seated him by mistake on a wasps' net; and the anguished journey, lasting for hours, in a bumping cart to a doctor in the neighbouring *moshava* [colony].

'My mother did not have an easy time bringing me up', he says, going to the bookshelf and fetching a framed photograph of her:

> Mother was beautiful in her youth, and with marriage felt that life had passed her by and that she had not lived the way she wanted. Too late she realized that my father – who was 15 years older than her – was not the man she should have married, and neither the place nor the work nor the conditions were what she should have had. She understood that she had talent for public service and self-expression, but had been ground down by the worries of daily survival.

He was a weak, sickly child, unlike his brother Israel, who was five years older than Yizhar:

> My brother was more like an animal growing of his own accord, charming and good and loving and a source of happiness and health. He was the beloved, successful son, active, helpful, generous, well dressed, good at sports: a football player, loved by the girls. I was the opposite – small and shy and plain and a misfit. I feel like that to this very day. But why do I need every-one to know that? Why stand on the roof and shout, I'm a loner?

– *'Actually, in your writing, you do stand on the roof and shout, "I'm a loner"'.*
'Right, but I'm the one who decides how much I want to reveal. You can have the deepest cleavage in the world, but you won't want anyone to see more than you wish to show'.

On Tuesday, 17 November 1942, his elder brother, Israel, was speeding on his Sunbeam motorcycle alongside the railway tracks near Ashkelon. He was purchasing land for the Jewish National Fund and his Arab assistant Hassan was riding pillion behind him, holding him around the waist. The train sounded in the distance and Israel thought that they would manage to cross:

> And they ceased and never came home again, except that each
> was brought back to the floor of his mother's home to lie
> wrapped in a sheet, a candle burning at his head, his mother
> choking, wringing her hands and crazy with grief.

As Yizhar described the scene in *A Story that Never Began*. 'It
destroyed my mother', he now says. 'My brother was the most
precious thing she possessed – more than me, more than her
husband. He was what she wanted but failed to be'.

*– 'When he died, was there some unspoken message, "Why him and
not you?"'*
'I was not close enough to her to be able to read any such feelings,
if they existed'.

The father, Ze'ev Smilansky, died heartbroken within two years,
and in 1946 Yizhar was stricken by the severest loss of all. Again, he
goes to the bookshelf and fetches a second photograph, this time of
a handsome young man, his curly hair-lock on his brow. His beloved
friend Yehiam Weitz was killed, along with 13 comrades, on 'the
Night of the Bridges', a Jewish underground operation to destroy
bridges used by British Army in Palestine:

> His death was like an earthquake for me – to this day I have not
> recovered from it. We shared something that I did not have with
> anyone else since. The ability to talk had been taken away –
> there is an emptiness within me. Now I have to recreate him
> within myself for us to continue the dialogue. Part of my other
> ego is the figure of Yehiam. We were even not alike, as you can
> see, he was good-looking, humorous, a charismatic person. After
> he died in this stupid military action meant to 'teach the British
> a lesson', I began to have grave doubts about the justification of
> Zionism, war, and our right to the land. Up till then I had no
> questions. It strengthened in me the feeling that no stone was
> worth dying for.

Birds of Paradise bloom around the entrance to his lovely house in
Meishar, a village near Gedera. Hanging vines and eucalyptus trees
in the garden, planted with his own hands. It is a spacious house,

white, very fresh looking, where the 80-plus Yizhar enjoys a second youth.

He was compelled to make the change, the result of an inheritance feud with his nephew, who forced him to sell the old family house in Rehovoth. Yizhar, who had grown up in the house and whose mother lived there with him until her death in 1977, refused to come to terms with the idea that the house would be demolished and the plot sold to a building contractor. 'When the bulldozers attacked my parental home, I shut my eyes', says Yizhar:

> We're living in a different era, money calls the shots, and each generation builds a home to its own taste. Today on the site of my father's house there is a five-storey block of flats, and instead of one family, there are 16, so perhaps justice was done after all. Despite my misgivings, the destruction of the house was not the end for me, but a most heart-warming beginning. I now enjoy the quiet life of the village, praying that I will no longer be around when the citrus groves that surround me, are sold and replaced by tower blocks.

His writing is autobiographical and expresses the collective experience of native Israelis. The colours, the scents and the sounds are those of the land of Israel – not just Yizhar's, but that of all the children who have grown up in this country. In all probability the bulldozer that flattened out his parents' home shocked him so deeply that it evoked his book *Preludes*, which deals with his early childhood. It came following 30 years of writer's block: 'I was sitting on packed trunks, waiting for the removal vans, when things suddenly erupted within me. I drew out scraps of paper, and seized by a fever, began writing on my lap', he says.

The loss of his home was, for Yizhar, what the petite Madeleine biscuit was for Marcel Proust: the screw that released the cork blocking his journey into times long past. Even though his childhood home no longer exists, his childhood will now live forever. Since then he has written several more autobiographical novels, all about his childhood and youth.

– *'For 30 years, when people spoke of "Yizhar's silence", did you feel under pressure?'*
'Very much so. The fact that I wasn't publishing hurt me more than it hurt anyone else. I felt like a woman who is repeatedly nagged,

"Why doesn't she get married", or "Why doesn't she have any more children", and no one knows what painful problems prevent her from doing so. The truth is that I had written a few things but they weren't good enough, and luckily I had the good sense not to publish them merely to stop the nagging. If I had died at the age of 55, I would have died in the midst of silence, but I lived on, and things ripened within me until there was a phase of elucidation. Fertility has its own natural cycle, when the seed suddenly germinates inside you'.

When the State of Israel was established in 1948, the political parties adorned themselves with writers, and he was elected to the Knesset on behalf of Mapai, the Labour party. He was convinced to do so when the party bosses assured him that he would have three days a week for writing. As a member of parliament, he fought against military rule over the Israeli Arabs, for environmental issues, and for national health insurance.

He was elected a Member of the Knesset six times in succession, and finally resigned in 1966. 'I didn't like parliamentary life, and I'm not proud of my political experience. I brayed like a donkey, drove my own bandwagon, and changed absolutely nothing, apart from annoying a few people'. At 50 he started as a first-year university student, continued through to a doctorate and became a professor of education at a Teachers' Training College.

He is an attentive listener, poses personal questions, and interviews as much as he is interviewed. 'And you, are you shy?', he returns the question. It's hard to judge whether this is genuine interest or his way of controlling the situation. A conversation with him is an 'I –You' dialogue. He is a hypnotic lecturer; they say his female students fall at his feet.

In his thirties and forties his protagonists were close to his age, but in his late seventies he began to relive his childhood. In his book, *By the Sea*, Yizhar describes a boy and girl awakening to love on the shore of the Sea of Galilee:

> She stood there, with all the shapely curves of her young woman's body. And suddenly she did things, slowly and with serene confidence, impossible to grasp until suddenly everything was complete ... she moved, the hair on her head catching the light, shining gold, flashing enchanted in the water, lapping at

the naked beauty of her young woman's hips, and the furry cleft of her rounded buttocks and her wide golden back as she moved forwards in the fullness of her sex, beyond the power of any tongue to tell her beauty, to describe how lovely she was.

– *'Do you still remember this girl 60 years on?'*
'Yes. I was mad about her. But, like Proust, I reconstruct my youth, live it again in memory, and grapple with it. Writing is the documentation of experiences that have not faded and the longing to say what has not been said. There are many layers of memory within me. First comes the concrete one, that you can describe and photograph, and then you can burrow underneath to the emotional layer and to my ego and all kinds of covers and reasons. I search for the precise word, like a musician before a concert tuning his instrument, not satisfied until the note is exactly right. Sometimes I add a small word, like a painter adding a touch of red, and if it's the correct word, it changes everything. I look for the right form of speech, to describe the passionate longings, what it is like to be a young girl and how her neck reflects the light. The right form of speech is covert within me, not fully fashioned, like an unborn fetus, it needs to be born so that someone who was not there can read and say: "Ah, that's exactly right"'.

He has known his wife Naomi, a painter and engraver, since he was 16, they married when he was 25. Women in his writing are dreamy, strong and fascinating:

> I was shy, a stay-at home, a bookworm. It was obvious to me I had nothing to offer, that no girl would want me. They took no notice of me, always preferring those with broad shoulders and a steady income, radiating self-confidence, who could afford to give them a good time.

In his entire writing and in his life, Yizhar was always concerned with the conflict between the individual and the group. His protagonists, as much as they wish to follow their conscience, succumb to group pressure and betray their finer ideals.

If he were in his twenties, and not in his eighties, he would have gone to Hebron, to join the Arab demonstrators, calling for the settlers to leave:

Nothing made of earth and stone is worth the life of one human being. I don't care if the City of the Patriarchs remains a closed chapter in history. Not one drop of blood – neither Jewish nor Arab – should be spilt over those Holy Sepulchers. Like salt and pepper, the Jewish settlers have sprinkled mines of discord all over the West Bank. I cannot forgive them their arrogance and feelings of superiority. The people they are dispossessing are, in their eyes, not human beings who have their own joys and troubles and needs, but black goats that have to be driven off the hills.

He is wary of the accumulating political clout of the Jewish Ultra-Orthodox parties in Israel: 'They must not be allowed to rule over Jerusalem', and proposes that we:

> ... separate from them, they do not represent Judaism, only one branch of it. They flout morality in the crudest fashion – in their attitude towards any one who is different from them. I believe that in times of peace, the Pious will lose their power, and the first to rebel will be their women, who are deprived of equal rights, and their femininity is considered a threat and abomination.

He still has a spark of public spirit that he struggles to suppress:

> Today I want to do what I do best, and that is write. Let the others take care of politics. I don't know how much time I have left, but during that time, if there are any embers within me, I want to create.

He believes that some people are born with a genetic defect that compels them to sing or play music, others are born with sorrow in their heart, and they will grow to be poets:

> It is innate, a congenital defect. Biography is the raw material through which you tell of the wound in your heart so that other people can know what you are talking about, otherwise you will be shouting voicelessly. The plot is only the occasion for describing what you wanted: the colour grey, for example, or nostalgia. I don't run away from pain and suffering, and I don't want the help of psychologists. If I were to be cured, I would be worth nothing, I would be a eunuch.

In his book, *By the Sea*, he asks:

> What remains in the mind of someone who knows that that's it, one more second and light will go out, and he will know nothing more of the world. How will it be? Just darkness? Or a great light? Or just empty and just, 'Please, let me, let me exist, God, let me exist', that's enough, yes, just to exist, that's all.

– *'Is this your way of contemplating death?'*
'I don't think about death and I'm not afraid of it. I can only regret the things I shall not see: the view through the window, the look in people's eyes. Now, at this time of life, there is something very tense inside me. Very tense. A kind of intensity that must burst out. It is important for me to remember life; important for me even to remember that you came wearing a striped blouse. I know that after death there is nothing, just as I know that there is no God, but there is something in me that every time has to check again, perhaps God does exist after all, perhaps there is something after death'.

## TRANSLATED INTO ENGLISH

Yizhar, S., *Midnight Convoy and Other Stories* (Jerusalem: Israeli Universities Press, 1969).

# CHAPTER SIX

# Yehuda Amichai
## (1924–2000)

# A Secular Prophet

Nine years had passed since Yehuda Amichai last published a book of poetry, and his numerous readers were waiting anxiously. He heard the whispers: 'Had Amichai dried up?', but bit his lips and moved on. When I asked him about it at the time, he said, 'Forgive me the comparison, but like children who hold their faeces inside and refuse to go to the toilet, so am I. At the moment I am consti-pated, and cannot let out what's in my bowels'.

Though gross and repulsive, the image was typical of Amichai. An unpretentious man, heedless to the great honours bestowed on him in Israel and abroad, he was seemingly indifferent to his being the uncrowned Israeli Poet Laureate. He often said that his family came from a stock of German farmers, and he was almost proud not to be an inbred intellectual:

> The highest achievement of a poet is to reach ordinary life, so never tell a poet to get off his cloud, but rather, to climb up to reality. In the nineteenth century, a poet was proud to declare, 'I'm different than you'. Nowadays we say, 'I'm just like you'.

And then, in 1998, as Amichai turned 74, his long-awaited book came out. He named it *Patuach, Sagur, Patuach;* meaning, 'Open, Closed, Open'. 'Life is a brief, closed interlude between two great, open plains, which are eternity', he explained the title, when I interviewed him in his beautiful three-storey house in Yemin Moshe, facing David's Tower and the walls of the old city of Jerusalem. That morning he had already swam at the nearby sports club, had gone for a walk and cooked a pot of soup. He said he loved buying his fruit and vegetables at the Mahane Yehuda open market. Everywhere he goes people recognize and greet him. 'Not because I'm a poet', he modestly said, 'but because I was a high school teacher, and most of them have been my students over the years'.

Because he had a young family, and children who could be his grandchildren, he lived the life of a man much younger than his years. 'I am like any other 40-year-old father, who waits up anxiously for his teenage daughter to come home from her dates', he said. Like a skilled housewife, Amichai prepared for us filter coffee and served yeast cake. He looked very fit, 'I've lost ten kilos over the past year, by simply eating half of everything. Instead of four slices of bread for breakfast, I'll have only two'. He passed on the recipe for yeast cake. As he was handling his pipe, he asked if the smell disturbed me. 'They say that it's less dangerous than cigarettes. What the hell, I'll only get cancer of the lips, and not lung cancer', he said. He laughed it away, like a person with not one worry in the world. All of this was so poignant just months later, when he was in New York: he felt unwell, went for a check up and was diagnosed with cancer.

In his book, when he still had no inkling of the malignancy that was soon to erupt, he wrote:

When I die, I want only women to take care of me in the *Hevra Kadisha*,
And do with my body whatever they find fitting with their beautiful eyes
And clean my ears from the last words I heard
And fold my arms on my chest, like the sleeves of a shirt after ironing ...

On the table in his study, lay a triangular stone bearing the word 'Amen'. Amichai said that it was a fragment of a tombstone from a Jewish cemetery that was demolished a thousand years ago, in his hometown of Wurtzburg, Germany. A Catholic theologian named Professor Muller gave it to him, as the pieces had been found embedded in the walls of a house.

I asked Amichai if he did not think it macabre, to have such permanent *memento mori* on his desk, and he said that for him the stone was an emblem of life; that he affirmed his life, the good and the bad of it, and said 'Amen' to everything. Defining himself as a happy person, he said that his poems helped him heal his wounds, which were mainly about love and war. In his view, we oscillate between two conflicting poles: the constant change that life demands, and a fear of the new.

A black and white photo of two embracing children caught my eyes: Amichai and his childhood sweetheart, Ruth, to whom he dedicated several poems throughout the years. A very pretty girl, and a gifted pianist, they were bosom friends from age six. When she was nine and riding her bicycle, Ruth was run over by a car, her leg amputated just above the knee. Awaking from the operation, the first person she asked to see was Yehuda. The nuns in the hospital told him to pretend not to notice the missing leg and to avoid asking about it, but the boy couldn't avert his eyes from the empty blanket. Ruth got better, and learned to walk on an artificial leg.

In 1935, when Amichai – formerly Pffeifer – was 11 years old, he left for Palestine with his family, just in time, and survived, along with all seven siblings of each of his parents, and their families. 'We are one of the rare cases when a whole Jewish family survived intact, we now amount to over 1,000 members'. Yehuda became immersed in his new life in a new land, and his letters to Ruth dwindled. Ruth's father and sister obtained a visa to America, but her handicap made her disqualified for immigration. Her father took her to Holland with a group of other German-Jewish kids, hoping she would be saved. But when the Germans invaded Holland, she was sent to death. 'She is my personal Anne Frank. I don't apologize for being alive, but she made me wonder if I could ever love an invalid woman'.

His Jewish Orthodox parents didn't reproach him when he told them, at age 15, that he had stopped believing. An incident from his boyhood in Jerusalem stuck with him: one day the science teacher decided to spend an entire lesson teaching the *Iliad*, remarking that the national epic of the Jewish people had yet to be written. Yehuda sarcastically asked if instead of tomorrow's homework, could he write the Jewish national epic. The teacher was raging as the class roared with laughter, 'You've always been a clown and a clown you'll remain for the rest of your life'. 'I think he was right', said Amichai:

There is something of the clown about me. I don't live like a poet nor do I look like one, and I have the child in me. Umberto Saba, an Italian-Jewish poet whom I admire very much, says that a poet is someone who keeps asking himself what is happening to the child within him. My escape route to childhood is always open.

In 1942, at the age of 18, he joined the Jewish Brigade of the British Army and served in Egypt. A mobile library trailer overturned in a sand storm, and the books were buried in the desert. Digging, he came across *The Faber Book of Modern Verse*: Eliot, Auden, Hopkins and Dylan Thomas:

I hadn't written any poetry before then, but reading through the book I felt like someone who sits in an exclusive restaurant and thinks that he can cook just as well. Those poems did not express me, so I decided to write my own.

I thought this was rather arrogant on his side, but Amichai got up from his seat to the bookshelf, and picked several anthologies in English, where he appeared alongside these distinguished poets.

Upon his discharge, he joined the Palmach and fought against the British Mandate. In the War for Independence, he was a soldier on the Negev front, and his fallen comrades continued to haunt him through the years, his elegies for the dead bearing debt and gratitude. He read Literature and Bible Studies at the Hebrew University; and his first book of poems, *Now and In Other Times*, was published in 1955. He was revolutionary in using a colloquial style at a time when poetry was highly stylised and artificial. Combining the new Israel with the Jewish past, his language simultaneously echoes both the Bible and modern-day usage. Subjects that seemed too prosaic for poetry became appropriate through Amichai. He coined new idioms and slang expressions, and his influence went far beyond poetry, and entered the spoken language, the texture of daily life and culture itself.

In 1963, the 39-year-old Amichai fell in love with Hanna Sokolow, a 24-year-old student working as a replacement teacher in his school. 'Coincidence became the fate that determined our whole lives', he said. Several months later he left his wife and baby son and moved in with Hanna. All of Amichai's books are printed and reprinted constantly by Schocken, his eternal publisher, and one of

the most popular is the bilingual *Love Poems*, which contain erotic
lines that he wrote for his first wife, Tamar Horn. They had a very
bitter, lengthy divorce. Was he embarrassed that those relics of
passions and feelings that have waned, linger on?

Yehuda Amichai smiled: 'Not at all. Poems have a life of their
own; no matter for whom they were written. Poetry fixes an emotion
in a specific point in time. It absorbs what you felt at that moment'.

The illicit love between Amichai and Hanna produced another
collection, *The Achziv* poems. 'Achziv, an abandoned Arab village on
a beautiful secluded beach in the north of Israel, was our refuge',
Amichai said:

> To this day I still write love poems to Hanna, I would have felt
> great loss had our love turned into a friendship. From the first
> moment it was a great love, ideal, romantic, precisely because it
> was earthly and not up in the clouds. Like love, poetry should
> be robust if it wants to survive. It's like the Bible, which even in
> a bad translation, one feels its greatness. I don't like frailty in
> any area. Fragility fits a museum, not life.

Amichai has also been the most popular Hebrew poet abroad,
translated into 37 languages. 'To my love, combing her hair/without
a mirror, facing me/ a psalm: you've shampooed your hair, an entire
forest of pine trees is yearning on your head', so read the
commuters in London and New York underground, between ads of
insurance companies and dog food.

Amichai's verse is communicative because of the universal
subject matter and the meager style, in which very little is lost in
translation. Still, he never considered himself a professional.
'Amateur is one of my favourite words', he said:

> I write about my private life, my loves, my losses, my aches and
> pains, and people encounter their own selves in me. I only
> write in retrospect. During love and war, one doesn't write
> poems. When cannons roar, you harness your energy for
> survival, and to overcome fear. Likewise, when you're making
> love, you do not stop in the middle and say to your beloved, 'I
> thought of a lovely metaphor; your neck is like the Tower of
> David'. Only at a distance, when you're not aware,
> things surface up. Art is like ruminating, when you re-enjoy the
> same things that excited you at the time of occurrence.

He never led a bohemian life, and his only artist friends were Ted Hughes and Allan Sillitoe. He first met Hughes in London, at the Poetry International Festival of 1967. Hughes was the co-director, and he read out some of Amichai's translated poems. The following weekend, Amichai, who was now separated from his first wife, came with Hanna to visit Ted and his lover Assia Wevill, at Court Green, Devon. It was the beginning of a lifelong friendship, and mutual admiration. Assia knew Hebrew, since she had lived in Israel in her teens, and Hughes suggested that she'd be Amichai's new translator.

A year later, Hughes and Assia, together with their daughter Shura, travelled to Germany and paid homage to Amichai by making a big detour to visit his hometown. Distressed and enraged by the fate of the uprooted and murdered town Jews, Hughes took out his pen, glanced to the sides, and quickly scribbled on the pink stucco of the Wurzburg Valkenhaus, 'Yehuda Amichai lived here'.

Hughes revealed that whenever he wished to free 'myself from my mental prisons', he turned to Amichai's poems. They were the ones he read most often, and returned to when he felt that 'the whole business of writing anything natural, real and satisfying seemed impossible'.

'Yehuda Amichai is my best friend', Hughes told me when I interviewed him in London in October 1996:

> He is one of the best poets in the world, and deserves the Nobel Prize. Every work of art stems from a wound in the soul of the artist. My wife Sylvia tended to focus on the pain, and to scratch at the wounds, while his poems are full with marks of pain and explosion, but also have a great healing ability.

Amichai did not show his poems to anybody before publication, not even his wife or poet friends. He said:

> I do not need other opinions; Time is my judge. I put my poems aside, and if after two years they still have the freshness of originality, I publish them. There are things that Time keeps alive and things it destroys. I never publish right away. I'm critical of my work. I have in my head a kind of computer that says, 'That's not it, you've said that before'. I really don't care if I don't publish.

One evening, as he turned the TV on for the daily news, he was

stunned. Scenes from a soldier's funeral filled the screen. A woman
was standing over her son's grave, reading from a small note held in
her hand:

> God full of compassion,
> If God were so full of compassion
> There would be compassion in the world
> And not in Him alone.

It was Amichai's version of *El Male Rachamim*, the prayer for the
dead. He was choked but not surprised. His poems have become
secular prayers for non-observant Jews; a substitute for those who
felt that the Jewish prayer book did not express their emotions.
There have been scores of such incidents. He got a call from parents
whose son was killed some years ago, but who had only recently
dared enter his room. On the table they found a book of Amichai's
poems, *Great Tranquility: Questions and Answers*. It was the last
book their son had read before leaving home for war. The mother
asked Amichai for advice, what poem should she read at her son's
memorial service? Amichai suggested, 'The Love of the Land':

> And the land is divided into cantons of memory and provinces of
>     hope, and their inhabitants mingle with each other,
> Like those coming from a wedding with those returning from a
>     funeral
> And the land is not divided into territories of war and territories
>     of love
> And he who digs a pit against bombs
> Will lie in it again with his girl
> If he survives for peace.

His poems are printed on wedding invitations, and read as vows
under the bridal canopy. An Israeli living in New York, told Amichai
that he read in one of his poems the following lines: 'Advice for a
good love: Don't love/ those from far away. Take yourself one/ from
nearby. / The way a sensible house will take local/ stones for its
building, / stones which have suffered in the same cold/ and were
scorched by the same sun'. The man left his American fiancée and
returned to Israel to marry his former girlfriend. As much as it
scared Amichai that someone changed his life because of a poem, he
felt a certain pride:

... because there is a preacher or a rabbi in every poet. Art wants to have an effect on others, to make people cry, or laugh. It gives one a sense of the power of the word, and I'm aware of the responsibility.

Another reader bought a book of Amichai's poems for his girlfriend and inscribed it with the words, 'Let the poet speak for me', turning Amichai into a Cyrano de Bergerac, a mouthpiece for love. 'In this case it did not work. They got divorced, and the man is married for the third time now. The poor soul must have bought three copies of the book already – one for each wife'.

Fleeting time and the inevitability of death have always been the subject of his writing; yet, in his old age, this concern seems more remote to him then ever. 'I feel like someone who has prepared his lament before death, so I'm ready for it whenever it comes', he said:

We all expect the worst to happen and are surprised when it doesn't. When I was young, I was more afraid. Now that I'm older, I've come to terms with the fact that everything comes to an end. Finitude gives value to things.

But then came illness. In the last year of Yehuda Amichai's life, when cancer had almost defeated him, Israel began to bid her farewell to him. There were numerous events and media celebrations of him and his poetry, as if the nation wanted him to know, in his life, how much he was loved, to what extent he was her secular prophet. Yehuda Amichai passed away on 22 September 2000. His tombstone, a sturdy Jerusalem rock, bears a quote from one of his poems: 'Even death will not part/but will join us, again, endlessly, in the universe'.

## TRANSLATIONS INTO ENGLISH

Amichai, Y., *Selected Poems* [trans. A Gutmann and H. Schimmel] (Harmondsworth: Penguin Books, 1971).
—— *Songs of Jerusalem and Myself* [*Shirei Yerushalayim Ve'ani*; trans. H. Schimmel] (New York: Harper and Row, 1973).
—— *Time* [*Hazman*; trans. Y. Amichai and T. Hughes] (London: Oxford University Press, 1979).

—— *Love Poems* [*Shirei Ahava*; trans. G. Abramson and T. Parfitt] (New York: Harper and Row, 1981).

—— *The World is a Room and other Stories* [*Barua'ch Hanora'a Hazot*; trans. E. Grumet] (Philadelphia, PA: Jewish Publication Society of America, 1984).

—— *The Selected Poetry of Yehuda Amichai* [trans. C. Bloch and S. Mitchell] (New York: Harper and Row, 1986, 1996).

—— *Even the Fist was Once an Open Hand with Fingers* [*Gam Haegrof Haya Pa'am Yad Petucha Ve'etsbaot*; trans. B. Harshav and B. Harshav] (New York: Harper Collins, 1991).

—— *Poems of Jerusalem and Love Poems* [*Shirei Yerushalayim Veshirei Ahava*; trans. A Gutmann and H. Schimmel] (New York: Sheep Meadow Press, 1992).

—— *Amen* [*Amen*; trans. Y. Amichai and T. Hughes] (New York: Milkweed Editions, 1992)

—— *The Early Books of Yehuda Amichai* [trans. A Gutmann and H. Schimmel] (New York: Sheep Meadow Press, 1994).

—— *Travels of a Latter-Day Benjamin of Tudela* [*Mas'aot Binyamin Ha'acharon Mitudala*; trans. R. Nevo] (New York: Sheep Meadow Press, 1994).

—— *A Life of Poetry, 1948–1994* [trans. B. Harshav and B. Harshav] (New York: Harperperennial, 1995).

—— *Great Tranquility: Questions and Answers* [*Shalva Gdola She'elot Utshuvot*; trans. G. Abramson and T. Parfitt] (New York: Sheep Meadow Press, 1997).

—— *Open, Closed, Open* [*Patuach, Sagur, Patuach*; trans. C. Bloch and C. Kronfeld] (New York: Harcourt, 2000).

—— *Selected Poems* [various translators] (London: Faber and Faber, 2000).

# CHAPTER SEVEN

# Natan Zach
## (1930– )

# A Gentle Man in a Harsh Land

When Natan Zach travels by train from Tel Aviv to Haifa, people gather round him.

> They think a poet, especially if he also appears on television, is some sort of minor guru, even if he doesn't cast out demons, sprinkle holy water or gives you rabbit's urine to drink. People in this country have a tremendous need to talk to someone, preferably a television personality, if not, a journalist, and if everything fails, even a poet will do. There are some who even want to confess to something, but if they were to make their confession to the Inland Revenue or their GP, they would find themselves locked in jail or in a mental home. They think a poet has some recipe for life, but I have no recipes for myself, how could I have a recipe for other people's lives?

The parents of a soldier who was killed in a road accident, asked his permission to engrave on her tombstone a line from one of his poems: 'I Want Eyes Forever'. He agreed. The Association for the Blind asked him for the use of that poem in their publicity campaign:

> They even, God forbid, wanted to use it as a kind of anthem. In their place, I would not want a poem that places so much

emphasis on their loss. But as they asked, how can I refuse, and not only because my own mother spent the last years of her life in a heart-breaking state of blindness, after suffering all her life from glaucoma – an inherited disease of the eyes which in recent years has inflicted me too.

His poems have entered the bloodstream of Israeli culture. 'Regret' was found in the pocket of Major Gonnie Harnik, who was killed in the Lebanon War in 1982. In so many memorial services in military cemeteries, his poem 'For Man Is A Tree' is read out loud:

Although I love that poem very much, I am not happy to hear it played on the radio, because it always follows a catastrophe. One day I heard it flooding the streets from the open windows. When I got home I turned on the radio and heard that President Sadat of Egypt had been assassinated. On another occasion it followed the death of General Moshe Dayan. After the bus bombing in Dizengoff Street, not far from my home, thousands of right-wingers assembled and shouted 'Rabin is a murderer', and then immediately began singing 'For Man is a Tree' in protest. But the poem was written in memory of the needless victims of the Lebanon War. If those right-wingers had known my political views, that I had banned the sale of my books in the Jewish settlements on the West Bank and in Gaza, they would not have sung it.

After he visited Gaza to welcome Yasser Arafat on his return from exile, and the two of them were photographed in an affectionate hug, the headmaster of a school in Beersheva phoned Zach to say that although he admired his poems, which helped him court the girl who became his wife, he had taken out all Zach's poetry books and burnt them in the courtyard of his house, as a protest. 'He also assured me that no books of mine would be allowed into his school. Actually I was pleased: at last, somebody takes poets and poetry seriously'.

A quiet house off Dizengoff Street...a curved facade in Bauhaus style with crumbling verandahs...an untended palm tree in the courtyard. Natan Zach's apartment is crammed with books, paintings and drawings filling every vacant spot on the walls: a portrait of Zach, painted by Streichmann; a painting by Tumarkin, bearing the inscription 'Elsa (Lasker-Schiller), a poet in Berlin, a madwoman in Jerusalem'. 'Our country of immigration is not kind on anyone', notes Zach.

The telephone rings. Someone invites him to the opening of an exhibition. 'I receive invitations to more than 200 cultural events a year. If I went to only half of them, how much time would I have left for my private life?', he almost rebukes the caller. So great is his popularity, that he feels persecuted:

> When I came home from a weekend in Haifa I found 16 messages on my answering machine, and I'm not even counting the letters in the mailbox. Only one person, Yoram Kaniuk, rang just to ask how I was feeling. All the others wanted something from me: to write a letter of recommendation for their academic promotion; to express an opinion on a manuscript. There are even pupils who ring to ask for an explanation of some poem they have been arguing about with their teacher. All they are thinking about is how to squeeze another drop of juice out of the lemon called Natan Zach. Twenty years ago I might have felt flattered, but today a ring on the telephone or the pile of letters in the mailbox makes me panic.

After not smoking for ten years, he now lights a cigarette:

> I had a hard year, and I'm not a man who turns for help, that's one of my blind spots. Sometimes I hide inside my own black hole and don't emerge until I have recovered and overcome the pain. I understand the mindset of those youngsters who travel to Goa or Tibet to find release or oblivion. My own Goa was the bars of Tel Aviv in the 1950s and 1960s. I have drank away years of my life in cafes and bars.

*– 'Seeking release? Because you are an introvert?'*
'To win the temporary illusion that man is born free and capable of choosing his destiny. And to seek release from the perpetual search for a "meaning" that will make sense of life. Today, I know there is no such meaning, and even the temporary feeling of release is imaginary. I may also have learned to live with myself and with the world without any desire or ambition to change it. The only pain that remains is the loss of friends or "witnesses to my life". I never imagined I would reach my present age, both because of my lifestyle, and

my destructive impulses. Even if one makes new friends – and I have a few, not many – one can't be consoled over those who are gone'.

Since the publication of *Anti-Erasor* in 1984, Natan Zach has not published a book of poetry, having used up his energy in political essays, the discovery of new talents and the editing of literary publications. He was busy in his academic work as a professor of Hebrew literature at the Haifa University, and generally in coping with life's burdens. 'From my father I have inherited light / and from my mother glaucoma and the intolerable difficulty of existence', he wrote in one of his poems.

Some people wondered, 'Has Zach dried up?' – but he bit his lips and continued to stash in a drawer the dozens of poems he had written in the past decade:

> If a singer doesn't record a new CD for three years, he is interviewed about his 'silence'. I haven't felt any need to publish a book for 12 years, and made no fuss about it. Even in the past, I never published a lot, especially compared with some of my acquaintances who already have 12, even 15, poetry books. I always wait for some profound need to emerge from within. I take great pains – perhaps too much – to let a book out only when I am convinced that there is something totally new in it. I have to admit that the attitude to poetry in Israel today is not particularly encouraging. But then I was awarded the Israel Prize for Literature in 1995 and like a good German-Jewish *yekke* I felt obliged to reciprocate.

This led to his 1996 book, *Since I'm in the Neighbourhood, On the Other Side of Sheikin Street*, which rapidly sold more than 7,000 copies. 'Almost a world record for poetry: apparently I was wrong about the number of people who still feel the need for verse'.

He has never published a poetry book without its being preceded by some serious upheaval in his life – leaving home, or a woman, or a country:

> And when I go, I perform a kind of surgical operation and leave everything behind me. I don't intend to write an autobiography, everything I have to say is in my poems. It's true that in my later poems I have exposed myself more than ever, but you must remember that there are very few 'verifiable facts' here. Facts are

not important in poetry – not to the poet and certainly not to
his readers, except the voyeurs among them. Facts are the fodder
of the journalist and the scientist. The poet is interested only in
the effect the facts have had on his life, his existence, his creativity. Not every man who feels himself to be no more than a living
cockroach writes Kafka's *Metamorphosis*.

Harry Zeitelbach was born in Berlin in 1930, the only son of an
Italian mother and a German-Jewish father:

> A kind of blend of romanticism and intellectuality, of a tendency
> to gushing sentimentality and a severe emotional asceticism.
> That is not a successful combination; the two horses pull in
> opposite directions. But anyone who learns in time to control
> them may find the contradiction useful if he is to be a creative
> artist. Thomas Mann explained his entire nature in the contrast
> between his mother, a pianist of Portuguese origin, and his
> father, the great, inartistic German merchant. My mother, too,
> came from a musical family and had me marked out for a career
> as a pianist or a composer. But Hitler had other ideas and
> decided: the boy will be a poet, and in the language of the Jews,
> believe it or not. And we listened to him.

He says, with that characteristic self-irony that he has elevated into
an art-form:

> When the Nazis came, they were rather polite.
> Father was well known, at least to them,
> my Italian mother was no problem, all they asked
> was to verify a few details. Everything according to the protocol.
> They entered the apartment and didn't even dare to sit down.
> But that very same night a friend phoned, incredibly, a police
>     officer,
> and warned us to leave immediately, preferably within the hour,
> for sentence of death had already been issued – because of our
>     wealth, as usual.

Natan Zach says:

> These are facts and this is what I did with them, though of
> course I don't remember any of them. Interestingly, the whole

incident was revealed to me only a few years ago, when a friend from Berlin suggested that we should go to the municipal archives and see what it said there about my family and the circumstances of their departure. After all, the Germans are renowned for their meticulous documentation and preservation of records. And it was true, in a file of the Ministry of the Interior, which I would never have imagined to exist, I found that a friend of my father's, who was indeed a German police officer, had warned him that hostile business rivals were plotting against him, and he wouldn't even be 'privileged' to go to a concentration camp, they would shoot him in some dark alley.

Only now do I understand why we were in such a hurry to leave – first for Denmark, then for France and Italy, and only in the end for Palestine. That's when I learned that my father was no great Zionist. All his life we never spoke about it, altogether my father never had much to say; just a few sentences a day. So I found myself in Eretz Israel, studying in second grade at school, without knowing a word of Hebrew. It was no picnic under such circumstances – that goes without saying. But who could you complain to, that, before age seven, you had been compelled to speak four languages? To this day I have a certain problem with this. Suddenly, for reasons I don't understand, something inside me refuses to move from one language to another, as though I would have to move from one country of exile to another. I'm also allergic to travel. It makes me feel as if I'm being expelled, or forced to do something against my will. Once a refugee, always a refugee.

He was pleased with a letter he received from America, from a professor of literature who had chosen the name 'Zach' for his newborn son:

But I was not at all pleased when I came back to Israel after a long stay in England and found that the telephone directory was full of 'Zachs'. When I left there had been only one Zach in the telephone directory. Agnon, for example, took out a patent on his name, but that's getting ridiculous.

He regrets his decision to shorten his original name from 'Zeitelbach' to 'Zach':

It was a bad mistake. Alterman, Shlonsky, Leah Goldberg, Uri-Zvi Greenberg, felt no such obligation. But my generation gave in to collective pressures, and we all changed our names: Amichai, Sivan, Avidan. Today it's a lost cause, since going back to calling oneself Zeitelbach, and holding to my father's name, would seem either a protest or a pose, as though only now had I discovered my roots.

Zach, 'a gentle man in a harsh land', as he once wrote in a poem, still has a heavy German accent after over 60 years in Israel, since his parents never learnt Hebrew. The innate foreigness and alienation, doubled during the Second World War; as a child of the forces of evil – Hitler and Mussolini – he felt accusing eyes stabbing his back:

My mother was Italian and they would make us get off
the bus when we spoke Italian
and German was even worse on the buses in Haifa,
and ever since I have had a problem with buses
and languages.

At 13 he had already published detective stories and crossword puzzles. He was an Intelligence Officer in the War of Independence, discharged with the rank of major. At the beginning of the 1950s he moved to Jerusalem to study philosophy and political science at the Hebrew University. With Arieh Sivan, Moshe Dor, and Binyamin Heruschovski, he formed the Liqrat [Towards] group, that paved the way for a colloquial style free of literary embellishment. It was modelled on English and American poetry rather than Russian verse, and was free from the prevailing Socialist ideology. They were joined later by Yehuda Amichai, David Avidan, Gavriel Moked and Dalia Ravikovitch.

Zach's first poems appeared in 1955. Like every great innovation, the book was received with curiosity and a volley of hostile criticism. In the literary periodical *Achshav* [Now] Zach attacked the verse of Alterman, with its symmetrical, mechanical rhythms, and advocated a more personal poetry, free from any institutionalized ideology, with a rhythm based on the spoken language. It has remained the central, dominant trend in Hebrew culture to this day.

'When I hear the hits of Shlomo Artzi, Arik Einstein, Yehuda Poliker, Chava Alberstein, Yehudit Ravitz and many others, I can clearly identify lines taken from my poems and those of other poets of my generation', says Zach, whose poems have been set to music more often than any other Israeli poet. 'And the best of the Israeli lyric-writers have also learned from us. We enabled them to deviate from the stock patterns of the Hebrew bard and to sing without cosmetics, in a language neither archaic nor pretentiously "poetic"'.

Already, before the Six Day War, he had published *Palms and Dates*: Arabic folk-songs, jointly translated by Zach and his friend, Rashid Hussein. He has always worked for co-existence and cultural cross- pollination:

> Because of the languages spoken at home in Haifa when I was young, with the coming and going of officers of the British Mandate alongside Arabs, Frenchmen and Italians, there was an atmosphere of Levantinism, in the positive sense of the word, which I pine for to this day. This is one of the reasons that led me to political activity – a blend of shared exile and nostalgia. To this day some of my best friends are Arabs.

To earn a living he has always worked as a teacher, an editor and a critic. During his 11-year stay in England, he completed his doctoral thesis on modernism, later published by Penguin. England has remained for him a second home, and if it were at all possible he would prefer to spend the rest of his life there. When he returned to Israel in 1978, he was appointed a professor of literature at the University of Haifa.

Many of his poems are written under a feminine persona, or have a female protagonist arguing with a man. His heroines are the porn-star Chicholina, Nana the eponymous prostitute of Zola's novel, or rape victims:

> In my old age I have become a feminist, but even in such early poems as 'Talitha Kumi' there was a heavy load of masculine guilt. God knows where it all came from. Some of those poems were written after the death of my mother and that is surprising, because until her terrible final years I never felt particularly close to her. I don't have a smidgen of unresolved Oedipus complex – Mother herself helped me resolve everything. Her illness, lone-liness, blindness and her despair must have made me more aware of the fundamental wretchedness of women who, in spite of all their hypocritical declarations and meager achievements,

live in a world dominated by men, some of whom behave like serial rapists. From the moment that women began to appear to my eyes as victims – even as my victims – I began to identify with that part of myself which is beyond salvation. This woman is myself, everything that I repressed when I emphasized the masculine element in me. Once I had become spiritually stronger, I could release that part of myself. Grandpa Freud could give you a better explanation.

He not only guards his privacy, he also keeps a distance from those closest to him. He's a lone wolf; during Jewish festivities, when families convene, he flees abroad, or hides away in complete solitude. He does not entertain people at his home, and cafés serve as his meeting places:

I write poetry only when I am alone, with no women, no friends, nothing – just music and a table. When life presses upon me – commitments, irksome duties and anxiety about earning a living – I do not touch a pen. I have attacks of writing, sometimes against my will, and then in the right mood 20 poems can get written at one go. And then they go into the drawer. My poems like to live in the drawer; maybe I too spend some of my life in a drawer. Only when the poems have spent a long time, sometimes years, hidden in the darkness, I take them out and read them as though it was not me that wrote them. And then, if they stand the test and haven't grown old along with me – I publish them. A poem is a magical combination of words, always 'anti-', always crueller than intended, an attempt to create in miniature some harmony out of destruction, a world in which there is no suffocation. Fortunately, I have a sense of humour, which helps me balance out the bitterness and the pain.

When he sees piles of old books and papers that have been removed from some vacated apartment to the street, he rummages, fearful that someone has thrown his parents' past into the garbage. 'I'm afraid of what will happen to my own possessions after my death', he says.

– *'Who will take care of your own manuscripts?'*
'The "Angel of Death" – actually, there won't be many manuscripts left. All the poems I have rejected, and certainly all the personal

letters, will be shredded. Anyone who failed to "research" me while I was alive will not do any 'research' once I am dead. Fortunately, I have never had any romantic longings for immortality. I have experienced eternal life today, yesterday and the day before'.

He is disenchanted with his life's work:

> If you ever thought when young that poetry could reconcile you and the world, you find out soon enough that poetry is an obstacle. It isolates you, wins you enemies and 'father-killers'. It fills you with resentment against a world that thinks it certainly possible to live without 'elitist' art and without a soul. The nearer you come to the gates of heaven or the undertakers van, the more clearly you see that poetry has mended nothing, neither in you nor in the world. I now feel that poetry that expresses only the pain and sorrow of life should not be published. Life is so bad, so hard, that poetry reflecting the misery of existence only makes it worse. Great poetry has never been, and must never become, self-therapy. Let the poetasters continue to express their agonies, real and imagined, and their own egocentric longings, but anyone who cannot add to the richness and profundity of life and enhance it with glory and beauty, let him stew in his own juice and keep silent.


## TRANSLATIONS INTO ENGLISH

Zach, N., *Against Parting* [trans. J. Silkin] (Newcastle-upon-Tyne: Northern House, 1969).
—— *The Static Element* [trans. P. Everwine and S. Yasny-Starkman] (New York: Atheneum, 1982).

# CHAPTER EIGHT

# *Aharon Appelfeld*
## *(1932– )*

# *Captured in the Web of Hallucination*

Even on the day that he learned of his acceptance to the American Academy of Arts and Sciences – that prestigious institute which brings together privileged members defined as 'unique contributors to humanity' – Aharon Appelfeld did not change his routine. He boarded the bus to the centre of Jerusalem, walked to the 'Anna Ticho' café, took his regular seat, spread his notes on the table and began working. 'A writer must not be swayed by honours and rewards, but concentrate on his work', says Appelfeld, the only Israeli writer beside Yehuda Amichai, who also belongs to that élite club:

> Writing demands self-tuning, and rituals make it easier for me. The regular hour that I have to catch the bus each morning, the view on the way, climbing up to the café, the welcoming smile of the waitresses, my table near the wall.

A permanent 'Reserved' sign secures his place, and a similar one on the adjoining table allows him uninterrupted writing.

Those sipping coffee around him do not imagine that the great tragic epos of the Jewish people, already unfolded in more than 20 novels and dozens of poems and short stories, is being written at the nearby table.

Several regular customers are imbedded in my books without their knowledge, not suspecting that I spy on them. I need live people in order to describe the looks and movements of my characters, just like a painter needs models. I borrow an angle of a cheek, a hand movement or a leg's shape.

After having won the Israel Prize for Literature in 1983, Appelfeld has been recognised as one of the best writers of our times. His novels have been translated into 22 languages, including Japanese and Chinese, and many doctorate theses have analysed his work. He has written all his books in cafés, his fuels having been coffee, cigarettes and alcohol, but now he sticks to mint tea in a tall glass. 'During World War Two, I experienced pain, fear, humiliation, and the thoughts are too agonizing to re-live them on one's own', he says. 'The joviality of the café balances my state of mind'.

Aharon (Ervin) Appelfeld was born in 1932 in Czernowitz, Romania (now in the Ukraine), the only son of an assimilated Jewish family; the father a wealthy industrialist, the mother young, beautiful and delicate. They spoke German at home, as Yiddish was considered commonplace. German culture was a substitute for religion in his kind of family, and gave them a sense of being true Europeans. Just like in his novel, *Baddenheim, 1939*, the Appelfelds vacationed in the fashionable resorts, looking for a non-Jewish pension in order to escape their noisy co-patriots. Ironically, and much to their dismay, they always found there assimilated Jews like themselves. A recurrent theme with Appelfeld is the self-deception of Jews, who deluded themselves that no one else noticed their origins.

'In all my books, I'm writing one story: 'A Hundred Years of Jewish Solitude'. At its centre is the radiating beam of the Holocaust, moving back and forth, colouring both past and future', says Appelfeld:

There was a naiveté among assimilated Jews, who thought they were the good and creative part of Europe, and all of a sudden they were told, 'You are the weed that has to be plucked out'. It was a terrible crisis, like pulling a sleeping person out of his bed, and placing him, naked, in the middle of a field. My books expose the process, from the peaceful life in the shadow of that radiation to the scorched earth. I write to give the murdered ones their names back, to redeem their souls and salvage them from the anonymity of mass extermination.

He was eight years old when his mother was shot to death near their house. 'I was "Mummy's child", very loved and protected. She was 34 years old. I am almost twice her age now, but for me she is still alive today, not a day older than 34'.

Professor Yigal Schwarz, Appelfeld's editor and an Appelfeld scholar, thinks that it is a mistake to label Appelfeld as simply a Holocaust writer:

The Holocaust for him is a metaphor for a basic existential state of mind, imbued in him from an early stage: the sense of never belonging, of never having a home and a family. The only warm bosom he knew was that of the Gentile nanny, immortalized in his novel *Katerina*. His father was always distant and estranged, and his mother occupied with her own affairs. Appelfeld mythologized his childhood, turning it into heaven and hell at the same time. In his early books, his lost mother is always described as an angel, and he was very harsh on his father, because he survived.

After the murder of his mother, Aharon and his father were deported to the concentration camp of Transnistria:

And then, one day, father was taken away along with a group of other men. I was ten years old, and people who were with us at the camp say that they can still hear my cries when he was torn away from me.

For 35 years his writing stopped short of the Holocaust, and he only dared to touch the fire in 1997, in his novel, *The Ice Mine*. It is the story of a group of Jews, who were slave labourers, carrying long, heavy wooden logs to build a bridge over the river Bog. In his spiritual autobiography, *The Age of Wonders*, Appelfeld described his father as a man who abandoned his family at a time of crisis, but *The Ice Mine*, dedicated to his father, is the beginning of reconciliation:

Hunger is the death prior to death. Hunger creeps into the bones and crumbles the soul, first, speech suffocates within you, your lips swell and your legs stumble. Not long after, you are wrapped in clouds of hallucination. At first, your friends do not notice that, and finally, when they do, they pull you out of it, give you a drink of water, take some of their own soup and add it to yours, plead with you and try to convince you that you must not become weak and surrender. There are people who love you and wait for you, and for them, it is worthwhile to live. Amongst other things, they warn you that if the sergeant notices you he will not hesitate to throw you into the Bog River. If that man comprehends the warning, there are good chances for his recovery. But in most cases, he who is captured in the web of hallucination cannot be rescued.

Appelfeld never researches for his books, and although this novel is based upon his father's experiences, he insists that he does not write 'about things that I am told or hear, but only about what I hear from within me and feel on my own flesh. All the characters I describe are manifestations of myself'. Since he was very young when the War occurred, and due to the processes of 'deletion' he went through while attempting to build himself a new present and to erase traumatic events, he hardly remembers any atrocities.

'A writer is measured by his ability to take his "Achilles' Heel" and turn it into an "Archimedes Point"', says Professor Yigal Schwarz:

Relatively early in his writing career, Appelfeld discovered his weakest point – the lack of memory – and turned it into his source of strength. As his memory was erased, his books draw a world that is doubtfully realistic, doubtfully hallucinated. The extensive family he created for himself, who represents all of the common notions of the 'Jewish tribe' in the past hundred years, is an illustration, not necessarily of what he had owned and then lost, but of what he never had. Appelfeld's protagonists are strangers in their own places, as he is a stranger everywhere. He demonstrates how the Holocaust is the single moment in modern Jewish history, in which all Jews linked instantly with their primal roots. The thunder that roared catapulted them into the core of Judaism. If not for the Holocaust, Judaism would have slowly faded away. The Holocaust forced assimilated Jews – like Appelfeld – to tie in with the past they had turned their back on.

Young Appelfeld escaped from the camp, and for three years foraged in the forests, sometimes alone, sometimes travelling with gangs of Ukrainian thieves. His blond, Aryan looks enabled him to hide his Jewish origin:

> Within the horror, I wanted to illustrate the humane sides of the Holocaust, great love, generosity, compassion. Even though a great deluge swept away all, and the Devil celebrated, there were nobility and compassion in the midst of it all. Apparently, selfishness is good for survival, but in fact, generosity is more useful. If you smiled at someone, a bystander saw your smile as well, and benefited from it indirectly. Every person who survived the Holocaust was saved by someone who, at some point, reached out or said a kind word. The moment you weakened and someone said to you, 'Your eyes have the most unique colour', that would have been enough to make you happy that he noticed your eyes, and that pulled you through another day. This is how I was saved, thanks to people who spoke to me, smiled at me, or gave me a sugar cube or a quarter of a slice of sausage. It was unusual behaviour at that time, as if one gave you a quarter of his own house.

In 1944, when the Russians liberated the area, Aharon joined the Red Army as a cook's assistant, and later hitchhiked for hundreds of kilometres back to the big, beautiful house he was born in. He did not find a single person there:

> Even though I knew mother was dead, I felt that both of them were expecting me at home, like parents waiting for a child, returning late from the playground. Throughout the war I imagined how happy we would all be once we were re-united, and I would tell them what I have been through. I often wondered how I stayed alive, because I was most certainly supposed to die. I had the life experience of a 40-year-old, if not older. I witnessed rape and murder and hunger and death, and nothing humane was unfamiliar to me. I was born into the world, and was immediately exposed to all of its faces. I survived against all odds, and I believe that it was love that kept me alive. I should have had severe physical and mental deformations, but I have none. My experience taught me optimism, because I understood that next to perdition and evilness lays goodness as well. Last

year, there was a gathering of Israeli child-survivors, and it turned out that each and every one of us paved his way, made a career and raised a beautiful family. And, after all, we came from the dunghill.

After the Holocaust, he was almost blind, not being able to bear the light of day, and mute, as he had barely spoken for years. In 1946, the 14-year-old Appelfeld immigrated to Israel all by himself. Educated in an agricultural boarding school in Jerusalem, he tried to transform himself into a proud Sabra:

> Naively I believed that action would soothe my memories, and I would flourish like the natives, free of the Jewish nightmares. The group dictate was, change, be taller, blonder, stronger, with bluer eyes. Write about the fighters of the Palmach, and if you came from 'there', then at least write about heroic Partisans. Ordinary Holocaust survivors were not *bon ton*. It took me years to draw closer to the Jew within me, and get rid of the prejudices I had.

He began publishing poetry in 1959. From childhood he had been attracted to cafés, visiting his father, who was an ardent chess-player in Czernowitz. When he was a university student, he escaped from his stuffy rented room to the Jerusalem 'Café Peter', which was frequented by Holocaust survivors, mostly refugees from the former Austro-Hungarian Empire. 'We all came there to overcome our loss, to sit together and conjure up our dead life. I felt at home among the refugees, understanding not only the Babel of languages, but also the innuendos, silences, sighs'. The café became his second home, a place where he studied for his exams, and made futile attempts to write about his new life in Israel.

> In that café I forever gave up the dream to become what I cannot be: to belong to something to which I cannot belong. The clientele made me understand that I could not escape who I am, and that like them I am uprooted from my birthplace, lost in my homeland. At a young age, I lost my parents, my home, Europe, and since then, I must surround myself with samples from my past, that I find in coffee houses. Every day I thank myself for refusing to delete my past, like most of my generation did. Many of them became distinguished army generals, going an extra length to blot out the 'Holocaust-Child' in them.

During his first years in Israel, Aharon Appelfeld never gave up hope of meeting his father again. Often he would search for his father's name on survivors' lists. One day, in 1953, already 21 years old, he spotted the name 'Michael Appelfeld':

> Someone led me to an orchard near Yavne, where the new immigrants were sent to work. They pointed at an old man who was picking oranges. I did not recognize him, 11 years had passed since the day we were separated, but he immediately recognized me, and ran towards me.

*– 'Were you angry with him for not looking for you?'*
'No. He thought I was dead. He could not have imagined that a ten-year-old boy, left completely on his own, could survive. We managed to bridge the gap of years and traumas'.

When war broke out, Aharon Appelfeld was just beginning school, and managed to finish only his first year, barely having a chance to learn to read and write. 'That is how Hebrew became my writing language, and I was spared the shock of switching from one language to another'. On completing his army service, he did odd jobs, spending his first salary, earned by paving roads, on a small typewriter. He still uses it after 50 years, each evening typing the handwritten notes he made at the 'Ticho' café. If he returns home after six hours with a 150 words, he counts himself lucky. He shuns computers:

> ... because the cleanness of the paper that comes out of the computer printer provides you with the illusion that you wrote something good. The typed paper will always be dirty enough for you to remember that it is still not good enough, and that you still need numerous drafts. And also, my old typewriter is a constant reminder of where I came from.

Appelfeld is a professor of Hebrew literature at Ben-Gurion University in the Negev, and with his wife, a pottery artist, has two sons and a daughter. Upon finishing a novel, he stows it away for some years like a winemaker, waiting for it to mature. He believes that the words should become mutually acquainted, communicate among themselves, and decide if they agree to the proximity that he has forced upon them. He needs a gap of several years to gain a neutral perspective. And, as he experienced everything before understanding its' meaning, he writes from the unknowing perspective of a child:

> In every book I write, I revive my parents, my home town, my childhood. And beyond that, this is the story of an entire generation. Literature aspires not to deface or obfuscate, but to clarify. I deal with clarifying things. Out of the mass that is called 'The Holocaust', I take a fraction of life, magnify it and show that these were human beings who dared, dreamt, strove, sent 'messages in a bottle'; so that maybe, on one of these days, someone will find their message. As I did.

## TRANSLATIONS INTO ENGLISH

Appelfeld, A., *Tzili: The Story of a Life* [*Hakutonet Vehapasim*; trans. D. Bilu] (New York: Penguin Books, 1983).
—— *The Retreat* [trans. D. Bilu) (London: Quartet Books, 1985).
—— *The Healer* [*Be'et Ubeona Achat*; trans. G.M. Green] (London: Quartet Books, 1992).
—— *The Age of Wonders* [*Tor Haplaim*; trans. D. Bilu] (London: Quartet Books, 1993).
—— *On the Land of the Reeds* [*Eretz Hagome*; trans. G.M. Green] (London: Quartet Books, 1994).
—— *For Every Sin* [*Al Hapshaim*; trans. G.M. Green] (London: Quartet Books, 1995).
—— *The Immortal Bartfuss* [*Bartfus Ben Ha'almavet*; trans. G.M. Green] (London: Quartet Books, 1995).
—— *Katerina* [*Katerina*; trans. G.M. Green] (London: Quartet Books, 1995).
—— *Unto the Soul* [*Ad Nefesh*; trans. G.M. Green] (London: Quartet Books, 1995).
—— *Baddenheim 1939* [trans. D. Bilu] (London: Quartet Books, 1997).
—— *The Iron Tracks* [*Mesilat Barzel*; trans. G.M. Green] (New York: Schocken, 1998).
—— *The Conversion* [*Timyon*; trans. G.M. Green] (New York: Schocken Books, 1998).

# CHAPTER NINE

# Yaacov Shabtai
## (1934–81)

# End of the Matter

He seems like the quintessential Sabra, his dark wavy hair curling up on his forehead, his pioneer blue shirt, laced with white ribbons, open at the chest. It is no wonder that the photographer, who was walking by on Mount Carmel on a hot day in 1950, chose to capture the handsome 16 year old, who had just been expelled for some mischief from the summer camp of the left-wing Hashomer Hatzair youth movement. The photograph of the athlete, who had won sport competitions in that camp, was chosen to appear in the *1958 Decade Album*, commemorating the tenth anniversary of the State of Israel. Prime Minister David Ben-Gurion admired the photo of the youth looking forward to the future, and had it enlarged and hung up in his study.

Three decades after it was shot, that same photo became the election poster of the right-wing Hatehiya [Revival] political party. They thought that the healthy, tanned youth, who emanated both power and compassion, would be a symbol of the New Israeli, and would boost their campaign message, that the West Bank Settler has taken the banner of pioneering from the Kibbutznik.

Yaacov Shabtai, by then a well-known playwright and novelist, and a lifelong supporter of the Left, was dismayed. The rise of the Right in Israel shocked him, and when Menahem Begin became Prime Minister in 1977, he was so vexed that his weak heart gave way and he was struck with a third heart attack; and finally succumbed to a fourth, fatal, one in 1981, aged 47.

The impending death with which Shabtai lived in the last decade of his life is in the background of his two great novels, *Past Continuous* (1977) and the posthumous *Past Perfect* (1984), which have been described as 'Dostoevskyan' and 'Joycean'. 'I cannot recall, these past several years, having encountered a new work of fiction that has engaged me as strongly as *Past Continuous*', wrote Irving Howe in his long, ecstatic essay in the *New York Review of Books*. Shabtai's prose, a stream of consciousness built of long, breathless sentences, had music of its own, like an orchestral score. 'The narrative hangs together and moves by means of association – mainly of characters, but also of time and place. The result is a thick but compelling literary labyrinth', enthused Alan Lelchuk in the *New York Times Book Review*.

'It was not an evolution, but a breakthrough in Hebrew literature', declared Professor Menakhem Perry of Tel Aviv University. It is unprecedented in Hebrew literature, for a writer of only one novel to be crowned as the greatest of his generation. Shabtai did not live to hear most of the compliments, since he died before finishing his second novel. He has had a deep, enduring influence on almost every Israeli writer since: here was the first exposure to the possibility of a totally different kind of prose that breaks barriers of language, grammar and rhythm.

Yaacov was born in Tel Aviv in 1934, the eldest son of Masha and Abraham Shabtai; to be followed by two more brothers, Aharon in 1939, and Yoel in 1945. The family would become mythicized in Yaacov Shabtai's prose, as would their home, a humble three-room flat at The Workers' Dwellings, in 15 Frug Street.

Their father was a foreman in building sites, a short-tempered, nervous, violent man. There was an ambivalent relationship of love, fury and bitterness between him and his eldest son Yaacov. The sons in Shabtai's novels always stand in the shadow of the fathers, engaged in some kind of struggle. Their mother was a self-effacing housewife, who channelled her artistic talents into writing beautiful letters. Yaacov was the apple of her eye, and he described her lovingly and longingly in his books, as the nurturing force, the Jungian Great Mother, installing dreams, food and anxiety.

In *Past Perfect*, the 42-year-old protagonist, Meir, sits in his mother's kitchen, devouring her Gefilte Fish and stuffed peppers and beef and apple puree and butter cookies, although his doctor

has ordered him to watch his diet carefully, since he has been diagnosed with high blood pressure and a weak heart. Meir sympathises
with his mother, who is sick of the house chores and duties towards
her tyrannical husband. Like the son, who hopes for a change of
place to change his fortune, the mother too wishes to leave everything behind and escape to the end of the world, willing to do even
with a small room and a meagre diet of stale bread, jam and some
olives.

> Almost unnoticed honey webs of closeness and fraternity
> enclosed the two of them as they sat together in the clean quiet
> kitchen, as if they were resting in a calm circle of yellowish,
> warm light, close and separate from all...and in a moment his
> father appeared in the kitchen door, and with a wide smile on
> his face declared 'We're going to Gibraltar', and waved his fist
> triumphantly, and straight away without noticing tore the close-
> ness and contentment which prevailed in the kitchen and had
> enveloped Meir and his mother. A bitter, though subjugated,
> emotion of anger and resistance flooded Meir, and without one
> word being said or hinted, he knew by instinct that this emotion
> was now flooding his mother too, who lightly nodded her head
> towards his father as a sign of approval; but in her expression
> under the thin layer of delight, there was something reserved
> and maybe even hostile.

The three Shabtai brothers were utterly different from each other.
Aharon Shabtai, who became a prominent poet and translator of
Greek classical drama, said that, 'My brother Yaacov was the handsome, the talented, the beloved, and I was the ugly one. I wrote in
order to be handsome, while Yaacov didn't even need writing, everyone loved him all the same'. Aharon Shabtai explains his sexually
explicit poetry as a reaction against their puritanical upbringing:

> I grew up in a home where it was forbidden to say 'cock' or
> 'shit'. I needed to be the bad, repulsive, perverted boy, to stand
> against the gorgeous and brilliant brother, and all that he repre-
> sented. The eroticism in my writing may be an attempt to
> expose the hypocrisy and lies of the sanctimonious, self-right-
> eous, Israeli Puritanism, which is expressed in sterile, ascetic,
> sexless writing. No Israeli writer, including my brother,
> regarded sex as a celebration, but as a sordid, dirty activity.

The youngest brother, Yoel, a gifted musician, escaped the constraints of the family and of Israel, and immigrated to France. All three became artists – possibly pushed to a dream-life of the imagination to escape the grim reality of their home.

Yaacov Shabtai was 16 and voluntarily working during his summer vacation in Kibbutz Merhavia, when he met Edna, a daughter of the founders. Four years later, she became his wife. The day of their first meeting, 4 August, would take on a special significance: in his play, *Spotted Tiger*, he wrote that: '4 August is a day of tidings and anxiety ... the sky was a barren abyss ... and he stood at the centre of the universe, before the open pit'. The 4 August 1981, would also be the day of his death.

After his military service, Shabtai became a member of Merhavia and worked in the pig farm, and when the kibbutz sold its pigs he became a teacher in the *Ulpan* for new immigrants and volunteers from abroad. When his plays received prizes – he gave the money to the joint budget of the kibbutz – he was exempted from a full-time teaching post, and was allowed two days a week to pursue his writing career.

In 1967, when the family decided to move to Tel Aviv, Shabtai was virtually without a profession and with two small daughters, Hamutal and Orly. Although he was a translator, playwright and a lyricist, and many of his hits were played on the radio, he could barely make a living. Once, two men from the Department of Income Tax Revenue presented a foreclosure writ and confiscated the refrigerator. Faced with this humiliating scene, his daughter Hamutal swore to herself that she would never take up writing as a profession.

In 1972, Shabtai's collection of short stories, *Uncle Peretz Takes Off*, was published. It portrayed a Tel Aviv that was forever young; a beloved childhood town. In the story of that name – which was later made into a motion picture – Uncle Peretz is a married man in his forties, who falls in love with a woman named Geula [salvation]. It is the story of a last chance, or maybe a first one, for love, even the most mundane things seeming wonderful with Geula. But Peretz wrestles with the immense, overpowering love, and eventually manages to ruin it and himself. At the end, he climbs up the roof and soars to his death, crashing onto the ground. 'Shabtai never perceived love as the major force that gives meaning to life. Love exists not in its realization, but in its absence, love cannot be achieved', comments his widow Edna.

It was no secret to the Shabtai family that he was having affairs; eventually having a child out of wedlock. 'We all knew about the other woman', says his daughter, Dr Hamutal Shabtai, a psychiatrist. Shabtai's protagonists have numerous affairs, they shuttle around between their wives and lovers, but love seems dull and pathetic, no source of salvation.

From the time of his first heart attack, at 36, Shabtai's daughters had to make sure that he would not be annoyed, especially when people came about matters of work: 'which was quite impossible, since he was extraordinarily irritable, and would explode in a matter of minutes'. As a writer he was a pessimist, and no wonder that his favourite book of the Bible was Job; but at the same time, with all the fears he was harbouring due to of his deteriorating health, he was funny and generous and talkative. His friends remember him walking for miles through the streets of Tel Aviv, one of them often bumping into him and accompanying him, engaging in heated discussion. Shabtai's stories describe actual routes that he used to take daily, the names of the streets symbolizing the protagonist's spiritual paths – walking from Brenner to Sheinkin, from Allenby to Dizengoff, actual streets named after famous Zionist leaders, writers and generals. His close friends became the recognizable models for the three protagonists of *Past Continuous*.

On one of these promenades, he told his friend, film-director Ram Levi, that writing prose was like sweeping the city's High Street with a toothbrush. Shabtai used to write endless versions to the same word or phrase, impressed by Dostoevsky who once tried 28 different descriptions of his beloved's eyes, in search for the exact colour. Shabtai used to consult his wife and daughters as to what combination sounded best. That experience would help Edna just a few years later, when she had to posthumously edit her husband's unfinished novel.

Shabtai was greatly disappointed that his first novel, *Past Continuous* [*Zichron Devarim*; lit. 'Recollection of Things'], was rejected by the leading publishing house Am-Oved; the chief editor dismissing it as simply a bad book. It was then offered to Professor Menakhem Perry of the *Siman Kria* literary magazine and publishing house. 'It took me a bit of time – about half a day – to realize that we had a Proust', says Perry.

*Past Continuous* opens with an all-embracing sentence,

'Goldman's father died on 1 April, while Goldman committed suicide on 1 January'. In the course of these nine months, the lives of Goldman and his two friends, Caesar and Israel, all in their forties, unfold: their parents and children; wives and mistresses; their achievements and disappointments; and death, which hovers above everything.

In the wake of the Six Day War, Shabtai lamented the Zionist vision and its sterile fruits: corruption and nepotism, soaring property prices, the rise of the Right. The three main protagonists are loveable pathetic losers: Israel the pianist, who strongly resembles Yaacov Shabtai; Caesar the Nihilist, who bounces between four women; and Goldman, who moves between different 'religions', from Taoism to dieting and exercising. The book ends with Goldman's suicide, and with a child born to Israel out of wedlock with his lover Ella.

The book was received in total silence, making no impact and hardly selling, and almost a year passed until an ecstatic review by Professor Dan Miron from the Tel Aviv University saved it from oblivion and made it a bestseller. As Irving Howe described it, the book represented the same breakthrough as that of Faulkner in American literature; the breakthrough that is made possible when a writer has complete knowledge of his people's culture, and can decipher the deepest, most secret sentiments.

Shabtai showed the chasm between the Founding Fathers and present-day reality that could not match the dream. The sons do not have the power and dedication of the Founding Fathers, and are crushed by the weight of their heritage, resulting in a sense of failure. 'The uninterrupted flow gives this novel its special character', writes Professor Gershon Shaked of the Hebrew University, 'The inevitable decline of the ideological aristocracy, that turned into an economical or dogmatic aristocracy, so that its sons cannot inherit it'.

In a radio interview, shortly before his sudden death, Shabtai spoke about his disillusionment with the implementation of the Zionist dream:

> I am frightened by the face of brutality, vulgarity, the boorishness and philistinism that spreads in the country ... I think it threatens the future of the land; it can bring about the destruction of the State.

'The social deterioration, is first and foremost the deterioration of the family and the tribe, which were the main knots that kept together Jewish society, both in the Diaspora and in Israel', observed Professor Shaked:

> The fate of the different protagonists testifies to the ruin. One has just to count the number of divorces and suicides in the novel, to understand that the choices of the author created a crumbling, disintegrating world.

Indeed, there are 24 deaths, including five suicides. Other characters in the book desert their families and go abroad, another form of disintegration. The monogamous family is broken by extramarital affairs.

Although not named, only represented as 'the city', Tel Aviv is an all-pervasive protagonist in the novel; but this time, Shabtai shows the deterioration of his childhood haven, making peace with it only in his last novel. Dining is another recurrent subject: 'Shabtai documented a society in which food was one of the only rituals left to connect people', in the words of Professor Miron.

As a girl of 12, Hamutal Shabtai was reading Freud's 'The Meaning of Dreams', the family were intrigued by it and discussed their dreams each morning – no wonder that she chose psychology and history in university. After a year, she decided upon medical school. 'When I switched to medicine, father was very happy. He said, "When you are a doctor you can treat me". He consulted me in medical matters, possibly part of my choice of medicine was to save father'.

In April 1977, just before Easter, Shabtai's mother died, aged 65. The fish for the traditional Passover Seder were left uncooked in the refrigerator. The father died three years later. The apartment was sold, although Yaacov Shabtai would have bought and kept his loved/hated childhood home, had he had the money. 'I do not pass in the streets where my parents used to live', he said in his last radio interview. 'My memory is vivid enough to see what was before ... Tel Aviv changes in such a way, that I feel like a refugee in it, a refugee in his own land'.

Shabtai's second novel, *Past Perfect*, opens with another monumental passage:

At the age of 42, shortly after Sukkoth, Meir was gripped by the fear of death, and that after he realized that death is an actual part of his life, that had passed its peak and was now going downwards ... and could be measured in measures of daily life, such as, how many pairs of shoes he would buy or how many times he'll go to the cinema, and with how many women, except his wife, he would sleep.

It all takes place in the late 1970s, when the social class that Meir's family belongs to has lost its political monopoly. In the figure of Meir Lifshitz, an engineer, married with two sons, Shabtai – who was now mortally ill – portrayed the feelings of a man whose body has become an enemy. The illness moulds Meir's life philosophy, until the only way out is succumbing to death and accepting it, the book ending in a mystic epiphany. Shabtai often complained to his dear ones, that the book was shortening his life.

Meir embodies some characteristics of the three friends from Shabtai's first novel: Goldman's death wish, Caesar's eroticism and Israel's loneliness. Like many of his generation, Meir believes in free love, but is too inhibited to do anything. He is embarrassed even to look at sex-education books; is terribly jealous of anyone who happens to be healthy; and, of course, of his wife, who succeeded where he failed, and had an affair. 'Meir is an individual who confronts his parents, his wife, his friends, the illness, death and God', explains Professor Shaked.

In the last weeks of Shabtai's life, he consulted his wife constantly as to the editing of the book. Nine days before he died, he leaned on his desk and told her, 'This book is yours'.

On 4 August, he went to bed, and asked his wife to massage his back. He fell asleep. Suddenly, he started to emit horrible sounds. His wife laid her hands on him, as she used to do whenever he had a bad dream. He opened his eyes and asked, 'What happened'? Edna Shabtai felt he was dying, and began to resuscitate him, with no success. She called an ambulance and he was taken down the stairs. Since his condition was critical, the doctor ordered the stretcher to be laid on the pavement, and to the blazing of ambulance lights, cut open Shabtai's chest and massaged his heart, but to no avail. A year later, the 35-year-old Dr Landes was killed in battle, in the War in Lebanon.

When Shabtai died, in the middle of the summer, and in the middle of the book he was writing, he left 1,200 draft pages. It took his widow and Professor Dan Miron two years to select the right phrases of each sentence out of the endless options that Shabtai had considered. They cut the manuscript down to 250 pages, and named it *Sof Davar* [End of the Matter].

## TRANSLATIONS INTO ENGLISH

Shabtai, Y., *Past Continuous* [*Zichron Devarim*; trans. D. Bilu] (Philadelphia, PA: Jewish Publications Society, 1985/New York: Overlook Press, 2002).
—— *Past Perfect* [*Sof Davar*; trans. D. Bilu] (New York: Viking Press, 1987).
—— *Uncle Peretz Takes Off* [*Hadod Peretz Mamrie*; trans. D. Bilu] (New York: Mosaic Press, 1993).

# CHAPTER TEN

# Dalia Ravikovitch
## (1936– )

# The Things to be Forgotten

A large, airy apartment in a quiet street near the Tel Aviv prome-
nade; dark-coloured upholstery; an abundance of lamps ('my obses-
sion'); a framed blue poster of a worn-out woman by Matisse; a
sticker for the 'Animals Rights Organization' on the bathroom door.
The television set dominates the living room: it is the lady of the
house's primary company, as she is alone most of the time.

One cannot escape her beauty. She is very delicate and fragile, a
fairytale princess, untouched by time: greenish-blue eyes, raven
black hair, carved lips, smooth white skin. Her voice is whispery.
She is a night owl: she writes, reads, listens to music until five or six
in the morning, afterwards she disconnects the phone and sleeps
until noon:

> It's a life style that began when I lived in foster families, and
> never had a place of my own. I had to save all my activities for
> the night, after everybody else went to bed, and the habit stuck
> with me.

On the wall is a photo of her father's eldest brother, who killed
himself, aged 19 while studying in France, following unrequited
love for a married woman. He was not the only one in her family
to commit suicide:

Miriam, my mother's eldest sister, and Levi Ravikovitch, were in love, and she brought him home to introduce him to her parents. She never imagined that he'd fall for Michal, her younger sister. It was a colossal tragedy. They got married in 1935, and Miriam, who was a spinster of 30, went to London to study. I was born in 1936, and the vicious gossips in our family say that I caused my aunt's death. Because Mummy, in her great bliss, was a bit tactless, and wrote to her sister how happy she was with this wonderful man, and what a perfect love-child I was. I read Miriam's letters, and I don't think mother ever realized how bitter they were. Miriam couldn't bear it, and ended her misery, but made it fatal for all of us: when a person kills himself, he kills something in those who love him. Mother was devastated; she wasn't so thick as not to understand her contribution to her sister's suicide. I was a baby, and remember nothing, but it may have had an effect on the way I was brought up. Whenever I sink into depression I think, Miriam, you had nothing to kill yourself for, my life is much worse than yours have ever been.

Dalia's father was an electric engineer and her mother was a teacher.

I had freckled fair skin and brown hair, and dreamt of being blond, thinking that blond hair and looks were beautiful, and I was sad that my mother never groomed herself. She came from a religious family with many children, and since childhood she worked hard at her father's dairy. After school she would run to distribute milk and even though she married a wealthy man, modesty and poverty stuck to her and was inflicted upon me.

On weekends they went sailing on the Yarkon River, her father was rowing and Dalia would sit opposite him on the bench. The 11-year-old Ahmed, the son of the Arab boatman, was her first love:

Every Saturday I would run to him and hug him and he could not really object because I was a client. Perhaps because of him I still feel an attraction to dark men with black eyes and velvet-like skin. I often ask myself where Ahmed is, and whether he is he still alive.

Paradise was short-lived. Her twin brothers, Achikam and

Amiram were born, and Levi Ravikovitch wrote a poem for his three children: 'I have a son and he is fat / there is also one who is thin / and another one a girl. / How can I tell between them / if the fat – got thinner / the skinny – became fat / and the daughter – short haired like a boy?'

> My brothers were handsome from birth, and I admired them. When they came along there was no room left for me, because they were two. I considered myself very unattractive, and felt great sorrow that from such a handsome father, an ugly daughter was created. Nevertheless I always preferred to be a woman, because a woman gives life, and I always felt sorry for men.

When Dalia was four, her father taught her reading and writing, and she felt that she had to be smart for his sake:

> He had strict standards. Once we visited friends and I fought with their young daughter. Father was shocked: 'You beat the hosts' child? Show me the hand that did that!' With the innocence and insolence of a child, I said, I can't remember which hand it was, and he hit me on both.

She felt court-martialled, and never forgot the insult. Years later she revived the incident in a poem named 'The Vicious Hand'. However, her father encouraged her to think independently, not heed to the opinion of others, and always believe in something greater than herself. 'For him the great passion was Zionism, for me, it is human rights, a deep empathy with the misery of the "Other"'.

In October 1942, the 33-year-old Levi Ravikovitch was ran over by the car of a drunken Greek soldier who was serving in the British Army. Dalia was told that he was only injured, and for her sixth birthday, two weeks later, she received a school bag and a pencil case, a gift from her father. Two years later, Dalia secretly confessed to one of her schoolmates that she suspected that her father was dead. 'What, didn't you know?', the girl exclaimed. Ravikovitch was left hanging by a thread. The slow permeation of the loss became her well of sorrow. Her poems to her father portray guilt and a feeling that no one, other than the father himself, can comfort her for his death. Since her father was a writer and left her a collection of poetry books, poetry became their common language in his death as well:

> And I had to fight for my autonomy, keep on living according to my father's principles, and become what he wanted me to become. He sent me on my way the best he could for a six-year-old girl, but he did not have the chance to raise me to womanhood. Had he stayed alive, I would have been a much more harmonious and self-confident woman.

> When I was ran over to death on the black road,
> I was beaten down to earth, in less than no time, contempted and frightened,
> And I knew in a twinkling of an eye
> That in all of the years to come like me you would be frightened
> And you will not beware of fire
> And not of a big wave at sea,
> And like me a hand will not hold you
> To pull you back
> From danger.

– '*Many writers (Amos Oz, Yona Wallach, Yair Hurwitz, Meir Wiezeltier) lost a parent, like you, at an early age. Do you find a connection between bereavement and the need for artistic expression?*'
'I do agree with the wound theory. Perhaps the wound is preserved within me and is not crusted until I heal it with writing. Every person who had a bad childhood began his life as a helpless victim, and when I write I turn an unpleasant situation of helplessness into an active process. But at a certain stage, like there is a law of obsolescence on felonies, there is obsolescence on traumas, and a person should be responsible for his own deeds, the trauma cannot be used as an excuse'.

– '*Do you sometimes feel that your father calls you to follow him, to the temptation and the eternal peacefulness of death?*'
'On the contrary, I feel that he is calling me to order and telling me to get a grip on myself. He is the inner voice within me, but not my sergeant major. There were several decisions in my life that he would have opposed'.

– *'You have made quite a few suicide attempts'*.
'Committing suicide is the result of an imbalance between the will
to live, and the desire to be released from suffering. The bottom line
is that I am here'.

During the week of mourning for her father, a school principal who
courted her mother when she was young offered her a job at his
school in Kibbutz Geva. Burdened with three young children, and a
fear of economic hardship, she accepted. 'Only ten years later she
consented to marry him, because like a typical Jewish widow, she
would not be consoled for father's death'. The years in the kibbutz
were a nightmare for Dalia:

> It was like living in the worst Gulag: hard labour, horrible treat-
> ment and terrible food. At age eight we already worked in the
> fields or cleaned our rooms, and I had aching hands, covered
> with a red rash. They despised intellectuals, even the teachers
> were considered inferior, because they did not do manual work.
> They humiliated and mocked everything that was good in me:
> being an excellent pupil, and writing poetry.

When she sent a poem to a youth magazine, hiding her literary incli-
nations behind a pen name, she was immediately spotted, and the
entire kibbutz made fun of her:

> I lived like a prisoner. I begged mother to let me leave, but she
> would not hear of it. Only when I was 13, did she give up and
> send me to a foster family in Haifa, who took me just because of
> the money.

She stuck out in town because of her spartan appearance, as the
kibbutz supplied her with only three skirts, one in blue, one in
khaki, and a floral skirt made from bathrobe material. When she
complained, she was told that silky clothes were only for the bour-
geoisie. 'But I couldn't help longing to dress up like those city girls,
and be as pretty as they were', Ravikovitch says, and her school-
girly voice still maintains the old hurt. Until her graduation from
high school, she went through five abusive foster families one after
the other. 'I remember one foster-mother saying at dinner, "and
now Dalia will tell us how her father died". Like a complete idiot I
did, not realizing that I could refuse her'. Her mother used to tele-

phone once a week but, although geographically distant, Dalia never felt abandoned:

> I am eternally grateful to her. She took care of me more than she took care of herself. I now live in an apartment that she bought, and throughout her entire life she supported me with a small monthly allowance that enables me to float.

Her army service was cut short, and at the age of 18 and a half she met the author, Yosef Bar Yosef. Between her second and third year of English literature and Hebrew linguistics studies at the Hebrew University, they got married. Three months later they were already divorced. A second marriage was also short-lived.

Ravikovitch's early poems appeared in Abraham Shlonsky's journal *Orlogin* [Horologe], and poet and professor Lea Goldberg read them and helped her get published. The first book, *The Love of the Orange*, published in 1959, made Dalia Ravikovitch an immediate maverick at 23, and she was acknowledged as a unique and powerful voice in Hebrew poetry. Her poems have a magical sensuality, a style that carries biblical undertones and an enchanting rhythm, and erotic forcefulness to the point of violence. 'A golden orange / loved his eater / loved his hitter / with all his organs', she wrote. She has received all the prestigious literary awards since:

> Writing is an irrational process that is judged by its results. I am not entirely conscious of what I am writing; my main theme is love, its existence or absence. My poems are my life, but I use disguises in order to protect other people who are involved in my life. The dates, the place, the people involved, are not important. I know what it feels to be hurt, so I try not to hurt others.

At 41 she bore her only son, Edo, to a man 18 years her junior:

> We all lived with my mother. It wasn't easy, because both of us tried to be mothers to the child, and we competed which of us was better. She loved my wretchedness and not my independence. Our view of womanhood was conflicting. I loved beautiful clothes, make-up, and being lovable, and she was just the reverse. She enslaved her life to mine. When asked how did she feel, she said, 'When Dalia will be well, I'll be well too'. As I

couldn't bring myself to part from Edo in the mornings, and I
also slept late, she would take him to the nursery, and I brought
him back home. Once she told me that people say Edo has two
mothers, I was deeply hurt, and we moved out. When you are
48, you don't want to live with mother, and you don't want to
live off her.

Feeling needed by her son, and her mother's loving care, gave
Ravikovitch a supporting lifeline. From Edo's birth until he was 11,
she had no bouts of depression, but she lost ground when she
decided to separate from her partner. In 1988, the district court
judge in Tel Aviv granted the sole custody of her son to his father.
Ravikovitch felt that her child had been kidnapped from her.

In her first 20 years of writing, she portrayed love as sensual,
sacrificing and total. From the 1980s, there is an ironic, bitter tone
regarding romantic love, and she switched from love to a man, to
that of a mother for her son. Her early poems are romantic, the
latter ones marked by satire and sarcasm. In the centre of her poems
is a speaker with extreme sensitivity, and deep emotional perception.

Depression has been her constant companion since youth. When
she is depressed, she says, it feels as though she has been sentenced
to suffer execution in four different ways: burning, stoning, choking
and drowning. She ceases functioning, loses her confidence, and
cannot even decide on trivialities, like going to the bathroom or
washing herself. 'The old sense of ugliness erupts all over again. My
genetics also has to do with it, depression ran in our family on both
sides, but a depressive heredity does not erupt without the catalyst
of a trauma'.

From the separation from her son, her mental state deteriorated
and she suffered one spell of depression after the other. In her
poetry since, she often writes about bereaved mothers of soldiers, or
about Sarah, the mother of fettered Isaac, using masks to portray
her enormous and wounded love for her son.

When I experience loss, such as the ending of love or the loss of
a child, I sink into depression. It is also a professional illness,
because a writer, who looks into himself and is activated by his
unconscious, lives at high risk. All of my depressions are reac-
tionary, although a stronger person would react less devastat-

ingly. When I am depressed, I am less than a fallen leaf. I do nothing; I hide from people, disconnect the phone and mostly apologize for having no energy. Had I had a normal childhood, perhaps all of this would not have happened. However, a six year old that loses a parent torments himself that, had he been a better child that would not have happened. Some people feel this way in adulthood as well, and each loss causes them an awful reduction in their self-image.

When the fire caught his body, it did not happen gradually...
And he kept burning with the power of his body
Made of flesh and milk and tendons.
And he burned for a long time.
And inhuman voices came out of his throat
Because many human functions had already stopped in him,
Except for the pain that runs through the nerves
In electrical flows to the centre of pain in the brain.

'This poem is about an Arab labourer, and the Jewish extremists who nailed down his door to prevent him from rescuing himself when they set his shed on fire', says Ravikovitch. 'If I had not experienced torment, I could not have felt the exploited man's tears, and understood the fear he felt before death liberated him'.

She has been a political poet, active in the Israeli Peace Movement, especially since the Lebanon war of 1982. Her poem 'A Baby is Not Killed Twice', evoked public fury. 'I always fight the establishment, because be it Right or Left, it is patronizing and abusive towards the oppressed'.

She fears old age, 'the falling apart of beauty bothers me less than the weakness, illnesses and loss of status that old age portends'. Dalia Ravikovitch concludes her book, *The Complete Poems So Far*, with a warning to the young poet:

And all the goodness that you will gain from this,
The best of all possible worlds,
Is a single grave that will be dug for you,
After pleading at the mayor's chamber,
At the cemetery on Trumpeldor street
At a distance of sixty metres
From Bialik's grave.

She has no illusions of resting in the old tree-shaded Pantheon Cemetery in the heart of Tel Aviv, close to the national poet, but expects to be in the new one on the outskirts of the metropolis:

> Because a poet nowadays is worth just a button. What pulls me out of the depression periods I sometimes sink into is not poetry, but everyday life, a slice of bread with butter and honey for breakfast, can scare off any sorrow, much more than the elusive poem. When life smiles at me, I can smile back. I always believed that a woman's role was to be a good mother and raise children, and that literary creation came from itself, and is less important than femininity. Today it is obvious to me that both are important, but if I had to choose one of them, I have no doubt that I'd give up poetry and choose motherhood and love. Fifty years from now, I don't mind if I am remembered as a poet at all, I just wish that when my son reflects on his life, he'll feel that he had it good.

– *'If you were to write your autobiography, what would you call it?'*
'"The Things to be Forgotten". Everything that happened to me, other than my poems, should be forgotten'.


## TRANSLATIONS INTO ENGLISH

Ravikovitch, D., *A Dress of Fire* [trans. C. Bloch] (New York: Sheep Meadow Press, 1978).
—— *The Window: New and Selected Poems* [trans. C. Bloch and A Bloch] (New York: Sheep Meadow Press, 1998).

# CHAPTER ELEVEN

# A.B. Yehoshua
## (1936– )

# In Search of Borders

His maternal grandfather Abraham, after whom he was named, was a rich widower from Morocco, who immigrated to Palestine in the 1930s with a son and two daughters. His father was a member of a Sephardi family that has lived in Jerusalem for five generations. The Yehoshua's son was born in Jerusalem in 1936:

> It was only reasonable that my mother, the new immigrant from Morocco, would pass on to her children a message of submission: if you want to succeed, you must conform to the codes of the middle class.

So says the prominent Israeli novelist Abraham B. Yehoshua:

> It's interesting how sharp are the instincts even of small children, who prefer the accent of their nursery mates to that of their parents, because they sensed that emulating their parents will hinder their success. My sister and I adopted the native Israeli Sabra values and behaviour, we shed our religion – although mother remained a practicing Jew – and studied at a prestigious secular school, Gymnasia Rehavia, which was predominately Ashkenazi. I have a speech flaw, hissing my 'ss', but my flawed articulation never marked me off or stood in my way, as would have the Sephardi articulation of accentuating the

gutturals 'Het' and 'Ain'; which is actually the original, beautiful, traditional Hebrew.

Abraham's father, Yaacov Yehoshua, was an Orientalist, the director of the Druses and Muslims Affairs Department at the Ministry of Religion:

> When it came to doing manual jobs like banging in nails, I would be the one to help mother while my father sat aside, no one ever thinking of asking him to touch a screwdriver or a hammer. I take after my mother, who was a no-nonsense woman; I'm very practical, far from the image of a writer that is lost in a world of muses. I take care of the house bills and accounts; I'm very knowledgeable and shrewd with financial matters. It is evident from my writing, which is not a collection of abstract ideas but made of very concrete materials, organised by a discerning artisan.

'Bulli' – his life-long nickname – and Tzilla, his older sister, grew up to be 'New Israelis'. They were both members of a Socialist youth movement, and Bulli's military service was in the esteemed paratroopers. He began to write aged 20, and published his first story when he was 21. Since his first collection of stories in 1962, *Death of the Old Man*, and his other early stories – 'Galia's Wedding', 'Facing the Forests' (both found in the collection, *The Continuing Silence of the Poet*) – he has portrayed the westernised Israeli experience, the well-established, 'Ashkenazi' life into which he himself integrated.

During these years, his father had been writing about the Sephardi way of life in old Jerusalem, and had published 13 books, but Yehoshua the son thought that ethnic folklore was demeaning:

> It's always associated with something weak, like a child that you caress on the head. Father was very generous towards me and rejoiced in my success, which is not easy when one's own son surpasses you and achieves fame. The reversed Oedipal competition was a creative stimulus for both of us.

After 15 years of short stories, essays and plays, A.B. Yehoshua achieved nationwide fame in 1977 with his first and best-selling novel, *The Lover*, which was made into a film. It is the story of an

Israeli family during the Yom Kippur War, told through several voices. Yehoshua wrote a breakthrough portrayal of an Israeli-Arab, in the monologue of the young mechanic who worked in the car-repair shop of a Jewish owner, and was secretly in love with his employer's teenage daughter and helped him search for his wife's lover who had gone missing during the war. The catalyst for the novel came from the numerous ads in Israeli newspapers at the time, placed by families looking for their sons or husbands who were missing in action: probably dead, but hopefully alive.

After his father's death in 1982, when A.B. Yehoshua's Israeli identity was safe and sound, he set out to explore his roots. *Mr Mani* was the saga covering five generations of a Sephardi family, going back in time from modern-day Israel to the Ottoman Empire, and told in monologues. In the middle of this great endeavour, he encountered inner obstacles, 'and almost threw away my notebook with all the drafts; so I stopped and began a different book altogether, about the heavy, apathetic Molcho'.

The slightly effeminate Molcho had been a male nurse in the army, and was in his element only when he could tend to sick people. Suffering from an inferiority complex, and deprived of human touch and a sex life during the long illness of his Ashkenazi wife, Molcho awakens to life only after her death, even falling in love with an 11-year-old girl. This tragic-comic novel portrayed a picture of Israel in the 1980s, torn by the disputed war in Lebanon, and the poverty stricken villages of Sephardi immigrants, and the rifts between different sections in society. Only after publishing *Molcho* in 1987, did Yehoshua return to his unfinished *Mr Mani*, which he dedicated to his father: 'A man of Jerusalem and a lover of its past'. *Mr Mani* eventually won him the Israel Prize.

> As long as my father was alive, the Sephardi world was his domain. He told me, 'You'll write your most important works after I'm dead'. I didn't understand it at the time, but he did realize that his death would liberate me and open some drawers in me. The dialogue between us had been enriched after his death, and I'm sorry that he didn't live to see it, he gave up on me ever touching my own Sephardi identity.

Yehoshua continued in the same strain with *A Voyage to the End of the Millennium* (1997). The protagonist, Ben Attar, a rich Jewish merchant living in Tangier in the year 999, on the verge of the second millennium, sets out on a ship to Paris, where his partner and nephew Abulafia has gone to live, after falling in love with an opinionated Jewish Ashkenazi widow. Ben Attar takes along his two wives, and the trip, and dispute between the two men, is also the rift between monogamy and polygamy, East and West, tradition and progress. This extraordinary novel is a drama of personal and ideological conflict about polygamy between two Jewish communities in Europe: the one at the heart of the Moslem world; the other at the heart of the Ashkenazi world. This colourful novel, full of amazing insight and historical precision, won a prestigious prize in America and is now being made into an American feature film. An opera is also being written, to be staged at the twentieth anniversary of the New Israeli Opera.

And still, when asked to declare his occupation in legal forms, Yehoshua never states 'writer', always 'teacher' – he's a professor of Comparative Literature at the University of Haifa. He has always placed his familial and academic duties first, and writing is 'a side-lane, a calling which defines me, but is not my profession'. 'Facing the Forests', his core work, was written at a pace of one short story a year. He always feels that he doesn't have endless time to sit down and write, so he must make use of each precious moment.

Many of Yehoshua's protagonists share his family history, and also resemble him physically, with their droopy eyes and slightly bewildered look, chronic sleeplessness and anxiousness. When growing up, his mother was determined that he should be either a doctor or a lawyer, and was never reconciled to his choice of literature. In the last years of his mother's life, Yehoshua had a belated chance to delve into one road not taken – medicine: several times a week he would go the Rambam hospital in his hometown Haifa, don a green surgeon's uniform and a sterile mask, and stand by the operating table. 'I had a ball when the surgeons invited me to watch, to learn how one opens a skull, or saw off a bone', he boasted, as we were sitting for an interview in his home. 'I'm not weak-hearted, not that I'll be happy to treat you if you were suddenly wounded, but I shall not faint if I see blood and bones'.

The reason for the crash course in medical training was *Open Heart* [*Hashiva Mehodu*; lit. 'Return from India']. Dr Benjy Rubin, the protagonist, has been dismissed from his apprenticeship as a surgeon, and had to make do with the less heroic job of an anaesthetist:

Think of yourself as if you were the pilot of the soul, that you must make it float painlessly in the space of sleep, and cruise without shock, falls or bruises. But you must also not let it take off and fly too high, slipping away to the afterlife.

Yehoshua writes. When the 24-year-old daughter of Lazar, the administrative manager of the hospital has been struck with jaundice during a voyage to India – a favourite destination with Israeli youth after their three-year army service – Benjy is asked to fly over with her parents and provide medical assistance on the way back. The parents secretly hope that the two young people will fall in love, but the promising doctor falls in love with the mother instead.

'Benjy had stayed in the operating theatre, but switched from the body to the mind', Yehoshua says. 'I'm puzzled by the question of "What are we, mind or matter?" That's the basic enigma of life. I do not pretend to solve it, but to shed on it one more ray of light'.

He thinks that too many modern novelists use psychological tools superficially, inventing motives and simplistic interpretations; for example, if the protagonist's mother had been detached, he would be attracted to hot-blooded women:

But even if we knew everything about the protagonist's past, we would never be able to understand his behaviour. Natural scientists, on the other hand, believe that everything is matter: electrical processes in the brain, so they think, cause even love. I try to show that beyond mind and body, there is a third entity, which I call 'mystery', and only bringing together the three of them solves the enigma of existence.

*Open Heart* revolves around the mystery of love that pulls, and holds, people together. The most inconceivable partnerships sometimes materialize, while the most logical and sensible may crumble:

Matrimony is the most intimate and the loosest bond at the same time. There's no freedom in the child–parent relationship, it is your son, and you're obliged to take care of him. In matrimony, one has to choose and maintain the tie constantly, since it can be broken any minute. I know of some couples that bore three children without getting married, because they wanted to maintain the option of freedom, and they are bonded together stronger than many married couples. In *Open Heart* I described a few styles of conjugality. For example, Benjy's parents, whose beds are arranged in the shape of an 'L', have a cool, civilized, detached relationship. In contrast there are the in-laws, Lazar and Dori, who are very close together, in a symbiotic, very affectionate relationship.

– *'Which one appeals to you the most?'*
'Symbiosis, of course. There's a lot of magic in being close together. If one chooses to marry, one might as well go all the way. If this model works, than it's the most desirable'.

Yehoshua reluctantly admits that Benjy's dominant mother is quite like his own. 'Through Benjy's relationship with his mother, I understood a few things about mine: her strictness towards me, her moral stance, her power, things that have blurred in recent years, due to her weakness and old age'.

Yehoshua, whom the *New York Times* labelled 'a kind of Israeli Faulkner', is a master of psychological novels, influenced by his closenss to his wife, Dr Rivka Yehoshua, a clinical psychologist and psychoanalyst. 'Just two weeks after we first met we decided to marry. Six months later, we were husband and wife'. They have two sons and a daughter. 'I'm a hysterical Jewish mother', Yehoshua says:

> When my youngest son promised to return at 4 am on Friday night, at 3 am I was already awake, waiting. When he complained that he was a soldier fighting in Lebanon, while I'm worrying that he goes to the pub, I would say, 'I'm making a living out of my hyperactive imagination, which feeds you as well, so you must accept that I would be up at night and fantasize all kinds of terrible scenarios.

He often feels sorry for Israeli youth:

> Immigrant parents are weaker, because they lack the language and cultural codes. Our parents' homes were deprived and sad, so it was relatively easy for us to break free. Our homes are abundant and happy, we are strong, well to do, with cars and computers and political views that are identical to our children's, we even listen to their music, so they have no reason left for rebellion. Our youth carry certain sadness, they are attracted to our warmth and strength and involvement, and their child-

hood lasts well into age 30. In order to break loose from the shell of home they need to have escape routes.

Yehoshua's family got used to discovering fragments of daily events interwoven into his novels:

> Sometimes you worry about their reaction when you give away family secrets, or insert in your book a friend of theirs, or an intimate conversation that took place at home. I sometimes feel that I have to make it up to them, not because of fame, which is a problem in itself, but also because they have to read my fantasies or erotic descriptions that portray practices that they would be embarrassed to think that their father knows. Some children refuse to read their parents works, mine were made to read some of my short stories in high school. When they had to write an essay and asked me what I meant by this or that word, I'd say, 'I don't know, go ask your teacher'. Now they realize that it's a work of imagination, literature is a chemical fusion, and not an admixture, you change the molecular structure of matter when you seize it from life and insert it in a work of art.

He says he's grateful for the Feminist movement:

> Thanks to it, we, men, were privileged to touch the real substances: in the kitchen, in childcare, literally in the diapers. There are all sorts of things that at first we were made to do against our will, and then we discovered they're a delight.

He believes that women's liberation is the key to any society's progress:

> Look what happened in Iran: the first thing that the Fundamentalists did was to imprison women under chadors, while men continued wearing regular clothes. If the bare body is a temptation, why should not men lock themselves away? Why make women the victim? Ten or fifteen years ago, my Arab women students would attend my classes wearing jeans, while now many of them are veiled. Intellectual Arabs know that this is a recipe for backwardness.

Arabs are intriguing protagonists in Yehoshua's writing, having a voice and substance of their own. In his early story, 'Facing the Forests', the Arab was a threatening shadow, in *The Lover* he was already a real figure, but in *The Liberating Bride* the Arabs are an integral, major and problematic component of Israeli society. Yochanan Rivlin is a professor of Oriental Studies in Haifa Univerity. Being invited to an Arab wedding at the home of one of his students, Rivlin enters intimate zones: sleeps in their beds, uses their bathrooms, trying to understand their psyche and their secrets:

> The book is about borders, between individuals, between husband and wife, parents and children, teachers and students, and between nations. If you don't have borders, how can you know what's right or wrong? That's the current cardinal issue, and the reason for pessimism, because today Israel is a country without borders. For 19 years, from 1948 to 1967, we knew where the enemy was and where we were. But since the Six Days War, it is all muddled, they are in our midst, we are in theirs. Jewish teenagers go to a discothèque in the centre of Tel Aviv, and an Arab youth coming from the West Bank explodes himself there and takes them with him.

Yehoshua has been named the 'Oracle from Carmel' and the 'National Conscience', and has been involved in political activity for the Left. He believes that the duty of a writer is to show reality in a different light, and consistently portray the moral angle and give a historical perspective. 'We were the oil duct that helped the peace process move on more smoothly, with less objections', he says, referring to Amos Oz and a group of intellectuals, as well as himself:

> When the majority of Israeli public opposed our views, even when 90 per cent of all Israelis didn't want to hear the word 'PLO', my voice was heard, I never felt hated or persecuted. *The Liberating Bride* says that in order to understand the Arabs better, one must address their emotional facets, their poetry and literature. I believe that literary texts hold very deep insights, more so because they are often unconscious. If we learn the Arabs' emotions, we may reach understanding.

But since the Intifada which began in October 2000, Yehoshua's views have changed: he thinks that the Arabs' demand for the 'Right of Return' to their villages deserted in 1948, is dangerous, impossible and unrealistic:

It will end in disaster. We would not demolish the home of an Israeli, in order to rebuild on it the house, which was evacuated 55 years ago. There's something infantile when a man of 60 that has left Haifa, Acre or Lod when he was an infant, puts his life on hold until he'll go back to the house he was born in. It is the way of the world for children to grow up and leave their parents' home, even travel far away to build their own. Why be stuck in horrendous conditions for over 50 years in the ruins of a refugee camp, and cling to an unrealistic, immature dream of going back to your parents home?

Yehoshua, an influential essayist, has said that the Jewish existence in the Diaspora is immoral – Jews are behaving like hotel guests, with no residential roots, always ready to leave. He says that 2,500 years of statelessness have left their mark, and although independence has brought normality to the Israelis, immigration is in their genes. Like recovered cancer patients, who still have a greater potential for a recurrence, Israelis have not uprooted the Diaspora from within themselves, and could again become Wandering Jews. After 40 years of writing, his artistic anxieties only deepen:

Whatever you did in the past does not shield you from the possibility of failure. You always start from scratch. Writers do not improve with age. Dostoevsky was the only one that became more elaborate from novel to novel. But my great mentor Faulkner, and Tolstoy and Joyce and Agnon, all suffered a decline. Experience and proficiency do not ensure you even the level that you have once achieved. I'm terrified of this, so I have to be vigilant all the time, driving with all the warning lamps on.


## TRANSLATED INTO ENGLISH

Yehoshua, A.B., *Three Days and a Child* [*Shlosha Yamim Veyeled*; trans. M. Arad] (New York: Doubleday, 1970/London: Peter Owen, 1971)
—— *Between Right and Right* [*Bizchut Hanormaliut*; trans. A. Schwartz] (New York: Doubleday, 1981).
—— *Early in the Summer of 1970* [*Bethilat Kayitz 1970*; trans. M. Arad] (New York: Doubleday, 1977/London: Fontana

Paperbacks, 1990).

—— *A Late Divorce* [*Gerushim Meucharim*; trans. H. Halkin] (New York: Doubleday, 1984/London: Sphere/Abacus Books, 1985/New York: Harcourt Brace & Co. 1993).

—— *The Continuing Silence of a Poet: Collected Stories* [*Shtikato Hamitmashechet shel Meshorer*; contains the stories, *Galia's Wedding* (*Hatunata shel Galia*) and *Facing the Forests* (*Mul Haye'arot*); trans. M. Arad and P. Shrier] (London: Widenfeld and Nicholson, 1988/London: Flamingo, 1990/New York: Syracuse University Press, 1998).

—— *Five Seasons* [*Molcho*] [trans. H. Halkin] (New York: Doubleday, 1989/London: Fontana, 1990).

—— *Mr Mani* [*Mar Mani*; trans. H. Halkin] (New York: Doubleday, 1992/London: Phoenix-Orion Books, 1994).

—— *The Lover* [*Hame'ahev*; trans. P. Sympson] (San Diego, CA: Harcourt Brace & Co., 1993).

—— *Open Heart* [*Hashiva Mehodu*] [trans. D. Bilu] ((New York: Doubleday, 1995/London: Peter Halban, 1996).

—— *The Terrible Power of a Minor Guilt: Literary Essays* [*Kohah Hanora shel Ashmah Ketanah*; trans. O. Cummings] (New York: Syracuse University Press, 1998).

—— *Voyage to the End of the Millennium* [*Masa El Tom Haeleph*; trans. N. de Lange] (New York: Doubleday, 1999).

—— *The Liberating Bride* [*Hakal Hameshachreret*] (New York: Harcourt 2002).

# CHAPTER TWELVE

# Amos Oz
## (1939– )

# The Secret Agent from the Eighteenth Compartment

Already, in childhood, his weak shoulders were bent under the load of his parents' disappointments, overpowered by the mission to fulfil the failed promises of their own youth. Although aspiring to be a university professor, his father had to make do with the mundane job of a university librarian. The mother, a natural-born storyteller who amazed little Amos with her tales, had hoped to be a poet, but turned out to be a reticent, melancholy housewife. In jest, his father used to address young Amos as 'his honour', 'his highness', the playful words nevertheless inculcating the notion into the boy – who at the age of five nailed the sign 'Amos Klausner, Writer' to his door – that he would reach places that his parents never had access to. The parents were an incompatible couple, and their son also felt that they wished him to make a *Tikkun* [a healing] in his private life, and have a better marriage and raise children properly. Accordingly, Amos Oz did become a professor of literature, a prolific novelist, a husband of 40-plus years, and a dedicated father of three.

He defines himself as the son of displaced people who were ostracized for generations in their countries of domicile. They moved to Palestine, not out of yearning for the Promised Land, but because they had nowhere else to go. In the early 1930s, when life for Jews in Eastern Europe became unbearable, his grandparents asked permission to settle in America. They were turned down. They applied for visas to Britain and France, and were again refused. A year before Hitler's rise to power, his grandfather had been blind enough to ask for German citizenship. 'Luckily, the Germans, too, like all the others, said, "We have already too many of you", and my parents were thrown to Palestine like a piece of dirt that Europe vomited out of her bowels', says Oz.

His parents had similar family backgrounds, but contrasting emotional make-up and outlook. The father, Yehuda Aryeh Klausner, was intoxicated by Nationalism, and ripe with modern liberal secular optimism, believing that tomorrow would be better. The mother, Fania, was gloomy and romantic, the sorrow of the world upon her. In their acquired homeland, they were also outsiders: secular in a religious neighbourhood in Jerusalem; they held right-wing views in a socialist country; and were city-people in a society whose ethos was rural.

Amos, their only son, born in 1939 in Jerusalem, was their joint image, far from the Sabra, the new Jew who had grown up in the land. Like his parents he felt an outcast; a pale, weak, wise kid, attending a religious school. He was a bit too diasporic for the pioneering ideal of the Kibbutznik, and on top of that, he was a poetic, daydreaming, magniloquent boy, when the demand was for muscular workers and fighters.

Amos was 12 and a half when his mother killed herself by gulping down an overdose of painkillers. His father withdrew into himself, soon got remarried, and Amos rebelled. 'I stood up and killed my father, and killed the whole of Jerusalem, changed my name and went on my own to Kibbutz Hulda, to live there above the ruins', he wrote in his autobiographical novel, *A Tale of Love and Darkness*. He changed his name to Oz – 'Power' in Hebrew – masquerading as a sun-tanned Kibbutznik; but, as much as he tried, 'I remained pale like my father'.

Oz was still a soldier when he published his first book of short stories, *Unto Death*; a maverick, soon to become the most well-known living Israeli author. He says that when he arrives at the Writers' Department in Heaven, and has to report what has he been writing about all his life, he'll say, 'about families'. 'For years, they prophesised the death of the family, but it's an institution that wears out ideologies and survives everything'.

He goes around in life like a spy or a secret agent. 'When I have to kill time in a café, I never read a newspaper. I'd rather sit and eavesdrop to people', Oz says:

> I hear a fragment of a phrase, and add a beginning and an ending. The other day I overheard two young women who sat behind me, and one told the other, 'Since I dyed my hair, he has not shown up. I know that this is not the reason, because when he was with Sarah, he didn't mind her changing the colour of her hair'. When I hear such exchange, I want to know who is the deserter, who was deserted, and who the hell is Sarah. And as I don't know, I fantasize. I have been playing this game since I was little, when my parents took me with them to cafés, and mom would say, 'If you want ice cream or corn-on-the-cob on the way home, sit still and do not disturb anything'. My writing career probably started in cafés, anticipating the treat. I would listen to people in other tables, and pass the time looking at somebody and trying to guess where did he come from; how did the room where he slept in last night look like; are these two brother and sister or secret lovers. I'm endlessly curious. I can sit for hours and listen to gossip about people I do not know. That's how I make my living, and I mean 'living' not only in the sense that I write books and get royalties.

He uses simple ingredients for his novels: love, children, death, provinciality, nostalgia, a bit of ambition; but he zealously guards his own privacy on these matters. 'It is a common misconception that if we knew intimate details about Gustav and Alma Mahler, we would understand Mahler's music any better', he reproaches me:

> The link to be explored is not between the writer and his work, but between the reader and the work. Good books are those that after having read them, I know more about myself. I'm not interested to know if the author was unfaithful to his wife, if he is promiscuous or disillusioned. I admit that there are some ties between literature and gossip, as the impulse for reading books, and for listening to gossip, is one and the same, but they are two cousins that do not greet each other in the street when they accidentally bump into each other. Literature is ashamed that she has a cousin that has strayed, and I will not have that literature will be prostituted too. As a writer, I want to draw a line between the protagonist's underwear, and my own.

Oz is probably the only Israeli author that for many years has been receiving a monthly salary from his publisher, Keter. 'It gives me freedom, but does not make me rich. I do not know one person in Israel who became rich just by writing'. He teaches Hebrew Literature at the Ben-Gurion University of the Negev, and several times a year flies abroad to meet readers:

> But I don't go to any country where a book of mine appears in translation, otherwise I would have to live in aeroplanes. I am surprised that my books are read even in Japanese or Slovakian. I would love to know how they are perceived there, how the reader's orchestra plays my score on the other side of the globe.

The morning of the interview has began for him, as usual, at 5:30, with a daily walk in the hills and valleys surrounding the desert town, Arad, that has been his home since he left the kibbutz in 1985:

> When I return, I have a coffee, and put myself in other people's shoes. Sometimes in the evening, I erase all that I wrote in the morning. I was never a woman of 45 or a lonely old man or a childless couple, but I try to guess what I would feel if I were. I would give one year of my life to be a woman for just one week, one month, and experience menstruation, conception, child-birth, breast feeding. My manhood deprived me of a whole range of things I would have loved to experience. Writing is an extension of what I would be if I were a she, or a different he. I don't want to stop being myself, but to contain more in myself.

*Don't Call It Night* is a story of the grand dreams of small people in a remote place. Tel Kedar – a provincial southern town not different from Arad – aspires to become Tel Aviv or New York. The local café is called 'California', the cinema 'Paris', the boutique is 'South Dizengoff Center'. 'They all feel that the real fun happens elsewhere', Oz says:

> I know the feeling well, since I was a little child, when I passed by a house and heard music, and I thought that real life is there, and I am the only one outside. Even today, I'm still filled with curiosity and long to be inside. We all have a sense of failure, as if the real action happens in another town, another bed, the neighbour's yard, and we don't have a ticket to that show.

Like Dylan Thomas' *Under Milk Wood*, Tel Kedar is a protagonist in the story, and Israeli voices echo in its space. Natalya, the
Russian cleaner, is a 17-year-old child-bride who lives in a shed with
her jealous husband, who threatens her with an ax. Tikky, a typist,
has borne a Down's Syndrome baby to a basketball player from Beer
Sheva, but he doesn't want to have anything to do with her. Pini
Bozo, the owner of the shoe store, decorates his shop with photos
of revered sages like the Lubavicher Rabbi and the Baba Sali, and
also with those of his wife and baby son, who were shot dead in an
random attack by a soldier, who had suffered from unrequited love
and went berserk with his machine-gun.

With thin irony, Oz tells of Muky Pelleg, the town Casanova
who sleeps around with every woman, although he would have
loved to be exempt from sex:

> Many people in this book are busy impressing other people,
> who in their turn are also busy impressing them, while what
> everyone really wants is to go back to the intimacy of home. And
> when they're home, they yearn to be out. I too move between
> these two poles. I decided to be a writer at age five because I
> wanted to impress the girls. The wish to impress, to communi-
> cate, still motivates me, but as time goes by, it becomes harder.
> When I was young, I wrote with full gear. Today, I lay a very
> heavy foot on the brakes. I fear a writer's block; I never know if
> I'll manage to complete the book I'm writing at the moment. As
> I don't know where it came from, I am not sure it won't be
> taken away from me.

In the small, intimate community of Tel Kedar, the inhabitants
reverberate with, and are replicated in, each other:

> I wanted to portray a hall of mirrors: a family, a town, and the
> connection of things that do not connect. The hidden strings
> between people, the inner game of reflections and echoes in
> groups of strangers or relatives. Sometimes a boy utters a phrase
> that continues to vibrate long after the boy is tragically dead. I
> cannot write music, but this book is the closest I could get to a
> musical score.

The dead are part of the town too, and the list of characters in
the last page includes not only the living, but also those who passed

away long before the plot began, their presence no less vivid than
that of the living. 'The dead are present in my life, coming and
going like ambulance sirens', Oz says:

> I live contemplating death. If the word 'religious' was not
> already taken over by fossilized rites, politics and national
> egotism, I would say that my books show a religious quest. It all
> has to do with the question of what is beyond life. The knowl-
> edge of death colours life, either in despair, or constant fear, or
> contemplation, or hyperactivity, wishing to make some noise so
> as not to hear the silence.

*Don't Call It Night* revolves around Theo, aged 60, and Noa,
aged 45, a couple walking hand in hand into the sunset. Their love
is intensive and total; a close, suffocating relationship, as Theo is
resentful of Noa's independence. They are not only lovers: but
father and daughter, mother and son, brother and sister to each
other. They have no children, and they look for substitutes in other
people, in work, in each other. 'Their childlessness makes their love
so possessive', says Oz. 'I really believe that a child bars you from
death. When you have a child, you have something to live for'.

In many novels, Oz plants the personal trauma of a mother's
early death, and the impossible life with the father, as the starting
point of a life that goes wrong. It is not accidental that so many of
his protagonists lose their mothers in tragic, sudden, unlikely
deaths, as if Oz the novelist could not let his creations enjoy the love
that was so brutally denied from him.

Noa is a pretty woman, a teacher of literature in the local high
school of Tel Kedar; a curtain of blonde hair hides half of her face.
When she was four, her mother fell in love with a soldier from New
Zealand who was stationed in Palestine during the Second World
War. The two left the country, but were devoured by a raging leop-
ardess. Orphanhood is also the disaster suffered by Emmanuel,
Noa's favorite pupil, whose mother was killed during a plane hijack-
ing. The death of his mother and the ensuing loneliness haunt
Emmanuel, bring about his suicide, and move the plot forward.

When Noa was 15, her father fell into an empty well, broke his
spine and was confined to a wheel chair. Noa had to nurse her
tyrannical, dominating father, and abstain from life. But the release
caused by his death when she was 32, comes too late: her childhood
experience sabotages her love life, and a faulty abortion leaves her

unable to conceive. Theo, 15 years her senior, a heavy, patient, authoritative man, nurtures her as a little child, buys her clothes, and lets her do as she wishes. Considering Noa's past, this placid love with a father figure is the lesser of two evils. She and Theo sleep in separate rooms because of his insomnia, but an eye is always open, as if there was a glass wall between them. He spies on her and she spies on him. As Noa is empowered and spreads her wings, Theo is afraid she won't need him any more. Quietly, he sabotages the project that is so dear to her: establishing a rehabilitation centre for teenage drug addicts, named after her beloved pupil Emmanuel, who killed himself. Theo pushes her out of the project, and as he becomes stronger, she weakens.

It seems as if Oz has created a Hebrew version of Ibsen's *Dolls House*, and has continued the plot long after the point where Nora left home. But, unlike the Norwegian Nora, who may still make an independent life for herself, the Israeli Noa will go on living with her partner, despaired, frustrated, bored, with occasional bursts of love that will sometimes shine through the curtain of clouds.

– *'You tend to bypass any reference to sex in your protagonists life'.* 'The sexual scenes are no different from any other scene in the novel, and two or three sentences are enough. I'm not describing intercourse, as I do not elaborate on eating, or on a sunset and sunrise. I'm not embarrassed to write about sex, but my taste does not include graphic descriptions of sexual positions. I do not give lessons in anatomy, and do not write sex manuals. I regard the reader as my partner, and he or she has to invest, dollar for dollar. If I portray sex or a winter night, the reader is supposed to bring in his or her own experiences to the joint venture. I do not want to save them the effort, and do all the work myself. I set triggers and invite partners to participate in the scene with me. Even as a reader, or an onlooker at sexual scenes in films, I'm insulted if some work is not left for me to do'.

Oz is very popular among readers, but the Israeli critics are extremely harsh on him. 'That's their job, to judge my book, and I won't swear at the referee, even if I think that I've been mistreated. The reader is a better judge than the critic, and Time beats both of them'. He says he would sometimes love to stop writing, 'But I'm like a Third-World woman, who is not aware of contraception. After every childbirth she vows that she'll never conceive again, but before she finishes the sentence, there she is again, pregnant'. A political activist, Oz draws a firm line between his essays and his novels:

> When I make up a story, the issues that torment me are not the turbulent present and the bleak future of Israel, but how can I describe the rotten apple in the protagonist's kitchen, so that its smell will emerge from the page.

Throughout his life, he has hovered around politics like a fly around a lantern:

> But I never sat at the helm, even when my friends did. I am sitting at the eighteenth carriage of the train, very far from the engine driver, and am constantly peeping from the window to see that he doesn't bypass the station, or is about to get derailed. I'm like a passenger in a plane flying over the Atlantic, not sleeping a wink, because he must watch over the pilot. From time to time I've given advice to more than one prime minister. They all said, 'Your thoughts are beautifully written', but disregarded the content. I wish that for once someone would say, your style is crap, one word does not stick to the next one, but your idea is brilliant.

In 1990, Shimon Peres suggested Oz as a candidate to lead the Labour Party. Life and art should connect somehow – this is the secret wish of Fima, Oz's protagonist from *Fima*, who lives near the prime minister's home and dreams of knocking on his door, chatting him up and taking him out for a walk. 'There's not one Israeli who has not ever toyed with the idea of being a prime minister. Me too. Peres popped my name with no deep knowledge of me. I know my shortcomings, the job doesn't suit me'.

*– 'Vaclav Havel was also a well-known novelist, a Nobel Laureate, before he became the president of Czechoslovakia'.*
'A writer is no worse president necessarily than any peanut grower or a film star turned president, but I'm not Havel. In any case, Israel would be better of with a woman prime minister. There's something in the archetype of a shrewd housewife that appeals to me in a politician. A woman would be a better leader, because she experiences intimately what a shopping basket is, a queue, minimal wages,

and worries for her son in the army, serving in the West Bank. She knows what it feels to iron his army uniforms when he comes home for just one night, and seeing blood on his clothes, not knowing whose blood is it. A man may also have the personality of a shrewd housewife, it is not hormonal, but a mental attribute'.

Throughout his writing career, he has used autobiographical elements in such a way that no one could trace them to their origins. In real life, Oz hid his mother's suicide even from his grown-up children. He needed 50 years of distance from the trauma, to feel that he didn't want to play hide and seek any more, and that he would tell the story as it was, in *A Tale of Love and Darkness*. Going back into his family history, and understanding how desperate and victimised his parents and grandparents were, he realized that he is the carrier of their fears and humiliation and, like them, is still standing with his back to the wall:

> The Jews have the right to be a majority in one place in the world, and stop being an eternal minority everywhere on the globe. The tragedy is that two nations, the Jews and the Palestinians, are locked together on this land, each with his back to the wall. But for me, the right for a home is unequivocal, and Israel cannot be a multi-national state, only a Jewish one.

## TRANSLATIONS INTO ENGLISH

Oz, A., *Elsewhere, Perhaps* [*Makom Acher*; trans. A. Oz and N. De Lange] (New York: Harcourt Brace Jovanovich, 1973, 1995).

—— *Touch the Water, Touch the Wind* [*Laga'at Bamayim, Laga'at Baru'ach*; trans. A. Oz and N. De Lange] (New York: Harcourt Brace Jovanovich, 1974, 1991).

—— *Unto Death: Crusade and Late Love* [*Ad Mayet*; trans. A. Oz and N. De Lange] (New York: Harcourt Brace Jovanovich, 1975).

—— *My Michael* [*Michael Sheli*; trans. A. Oz and N. De Lange] (London: Chatto and Windus, 1976).

—— *The Hill of Evil Counsel: Three Stories* [*Har Haetza Hara'a*; trans. A. Oz and N. De Lange] (New York: Harcourt Brace Jovanovich, 1978, 1991).

—— *Soumchi* [*Soumchi*; trans. P. Farmer] (London: HarperCollins Children's Books, 1980).

—— *In the Land of Israel: Political and Social Views* [*Po Vesham Be'eretz Israel*; trans. M. Goldberg-Bartura] (London: Fontana Paperbacks, 1985).

—— *Black Box* [*Kufsa Schora*; trans. A. Oz and N. De Lange] (New York: Vintage International, 1988).

—— *To Know a Woman* [*Lada'at Isha*; trans. N. De Lange] (San Diego, CA: Harcourt Brace Jovanovich, 1991, 1997).

—— *Where the Jackals Howl: and Other Stories* [*Artzot Hatan*; trans. N. De Lange and P. Simpson] (London: Vintage, 1992).

—— *A Perfect Peace* [*Menucha Nechona*; trans. H. Halkin] (London/New York: Vintage/Harcourt Brace Jovanovich, 1993).

—— *Fima* [*Hamatzav Hashlishi*; trans. N. De Lange] (London: Vintage, 1994/New York: Harcourt Brace Jovanovich, 1996).

—— *Under This Blazing Light: Essays* [*Beor Hatchelet Ha'aza*; trans. N. De Lange] (Cambridge: Press Syndicate of the University of Cambridge, 1995).

—— *Don't Call It Night* [*Al Tagidi Layla*; trans. N. De Lange] (London: Chatto and Windus, 1995/New York: Harcourt Brace Jovanovich, 1996).

—— *Panther in the Basement* [*Panther Bamartef*; trans. N. De Lange] (London: Vintage, 1997/New York: Harcourt Brace Jovanovich, 1998).

—— *The Same Sea: A Novel in Verse* [*Otto Hayam*; trans. N. De Lange] (New York: Harcourt Brace Jovanovich, 2001/London: Vintage, 2002).

# CHAPTER THIRTEEN

# Hannah Bat-Shahar
## (1944– )

# The Double Life of the Rabbi's Wife

It was obvious I couldn't come to her home, read her real name on the door, take a peep into her life. When we were groping our way on the telephone, trying to find a possible meeting-place, I stifled my surprise when she tossed out the names of fashionable, bohemian Jerusalem cafés. We didn't fix on any means of identification; I knew her appearance would give her away.

After several hours of conversation, as night was falling and a slight chill came through the vaulted stone windows of the café overlooking the twinkling lights of Mount Zion, Hannah Bat-Shahar adjusted her wig, moving the blonde hair on her forehead, and said:

> I feel like a walking mask: this wig is a mask; these long, all-covering clothes are a disguise; and I'm hiding behind an assumed name. Even I don't always know who I am; my feelings, my desires, my yearnings, are all hidden.

In Ultra-Orthodox society she is known as the wife of a highly respected, admired rabbi, an exemplary woman, a do-gooder. 'No one suspects my destructive side'. No one knows that she is an author, her woman friends have never read her stories, never heard the name 'Bat-Shahar'. If it were revealed, the pious society to which she belongs would boycott and ostracize her children. Her daughters won't find a good match, 'For how could they be decent, if they were brought up by such a mother. People would whisper behind my husband's back, poor man, his wife is deranged'.

Since she first published in 1989, she has never missed a reading or a cultural event, hence her familiarity with literary Jerusalem. No, she is not afraid of being recognized here. People from her circles do not frequent these places.

She was an exceptional child and, at 13, sublimated her yearnings by writing romantic novels in which the young heroines married their heart's desire:

> I was good at essay writing, but my teachers frowned upon my independent ideas. Luckily, my father did not restrict my reading, and I borrowed books from the public libraries, and read *War and Peace*, *Crime and Punishment*, and *Madame Bovary*. People in my society would blame my transgression on my parents, who failed to prevent me from forbidden literature.

Bat-Shahar admired her father – a wise, authoritative man. In some of her stories there is a markedly erotic father figure whose presence prevents his daughter from loving another man:

> I regretted not being born a boy. A girl is not allowed to say the blessings on the Torah, and is deprived of what the Ultra-Orthodox world offers boys. I so much wanted to be like a boy, I would smash keys with a blow from my fist, to demonstrate how strong I was. All my life I felt that if I had been a boy, my father would have been more satisfied with me. I am not sure I would have dared to publish a book if he were still alive.

Hannah Bat-Shahar participated in a workshop for creative writing held at Bet HaSofer, Writers' House, and gained fame with *Calling the Bats* – six stories that focus on a fierce desire for love, verging upon incest. Her protagonists do not have a markedly religious background; she rarely describes them wearing a *kipa* or lighting Shabbat candles. Most of the names, though, are old-fashioned: Leah, Riva, Manya. 'Those are the names I know and circumscribe me', she says.

There are always women at the centre of her stories, haunted by guilt feelings, struggling with impulses that finally break free. 'Once I tried to write from the point of view of a man and he turned out a very womanly man', she says. She writes with a pen, at least seven drafts for each story:

> My best ideas come to me when I'm cleaning the house or cooking. That's why I don't want any help; the maid would only be in my way when I follow the urge to write. When the lines come to me, I can leave the onions frying on the stove and run to the page. It's worst on Shabbat, when sentences explode in my head, but it is forbidden to write. I memorize them over and over, and count the words, so that I can reconstruct the whole phrase later. I impatiently wait to see the first three stars in the sky, to signal the end of the Shabbat, and rush to my notebook.

The family is the pivot of all her stories. 'Unlike other Israeli authors, I ignore wars and politics. My concern is with the need of a woman for another woman, of woman for a man, and all the various combinations and permutations'.

Her second book, *The Butterfly Dance* – published by Keter in 1993 – is a collection of four novellas with the recurrent motives of an early love that never came to fruition and continues to affect the life of the protagonist. Wretched marriages, mothers who do not love their children, women who are handicapped, ill or inadequate in some way: 'I dramatize myself through my characters. It's a kind of inner theater where I stage plays and allow my characters to clash and interact'.

The story *Sacrifice*, begins with the childhood love of a step-brother and sister. She keeps his pledge of love in her heart, even after she marries a man several years older than herself, by whom she has a daughter. Life separates the childhood lovers; the step-brother leaves for the USA, marries and is widowed at a young age. When he rings his stepsister and asks if his son can stay with her in Israel, she fantasizes that this is an attempt to renew the romantic relationship that was never materialized. Her encounter with the son, who could have been her own child, proves to her that her life is a failure of missed opportunities. Something prohibits all of Bat-Shahar's heroines from living a full life, being happy, breaking out of the passive circle in which they live.

Bat-Shahar revived the memory of her own love for a cousin, whom she met at her grandmother's home during the summer holidays when they were both teenagers:

We used to go to the sea together and I was crazy about him. He doesn't know to this day that I was in love with him, and he certainly wasn't worthy of my feelings. One often falls in love with a figment of the imagination, not with a real person. Although nothing physical happened between us, the relationship touched on incest. Thoughts of transgression are worse than the transgression itself. All my life I have kept this unrequited love of my youth locked up inside me, and the longings have remained, they always remain. All my heroines are motivated by loss and the desire for consolation. My own consolation is in writing. Perhaps I should have said that my consolation is my husband, but we each lead a life of our own.

She loves and respects her husband, but her soul hovers in other worlds. Theirs was an arranged marriage, when she was 20 years old:

I have told him several times, that he deserves a better wife than me. He should have had a simple, pious, warm, unproblematic woman, who can give love, and not be an egocentric like me, immersed in herself. Writing is a very narcissistic activity. As a writer I am looking at my own reflection all the time. My unfortunate husband! I told him once it's a pity we aren't still living in the times of the Patriarchs, when every man had two or three wives. The others would take care of him and serve him as a true spouse should, and I could be relaxed and devote myself with no qualms of conscience to the only thing that really interests me, my writing. I should have been an ordinary, contented woman satisfied with family life, but I'm not. Nothing, not my children, nor my husband, gives me such joy as writing, it is my only satisfaction in life. If I were not to write, I would simply die.

Her husband, who saw her filling notebook after notebook, consoled himself that she was just scribbling for her own amusement. Her children too had no idea what was occupying their mother for hours on end. If anyone approached, she would instinctively cover the page. Only one of her closest friends was privy to the secret:

When I was looking for a pen name that would not give me away, my friend suggested Bat-Shahar ['Daughter of Dawn'].

Today, I would prefer to be called just Hannah, like the
Orthodox poet who called herself Zelda. 'Bat-Shahar' has a
Canaanite ring about it that doesn't suit me. The world I
describe is much more 'Yiddishist'.

When *Calling the Bats* was published, she emerged slightly from
her self-imposed seclusion. She had to tell her family that she had
published a book because, as a housewife, she had to explain the
mysterious income: royalties from the publisher. It still remains a
complete secret from the neighbourhood. The members of her
congregation and her married children's in-laws must not know
about it:

It would cast a slur on all of us. Zelda's family suffered badly
when her writings were published. Her poems, although full of
faith, are not taught in religious schools. There is no chance that
anything I have written could ever find a place in an anthology
for religious students.

She keeps copies of her own books deeply hidden in a cupboard
by her bed, where no one can find them. Her husband has not read
them, and never will:

It's only because I know that he will not read a line of mine that
I can be so outspoken in my writing. I don't want to hurt him.
He is a wonderful, good-hearted man. If he were to read my
stories, they would reveal to him very unpleasant things about
his wife; my heroines dream of other men, they are disappointed
with their own lives, and I am afraid he would find something
of me in every one of them. If he read me and knew my inner
world, we could be closer emotionally, but then, it might be
difficult for us to remain in our community, which is very dear
to me.

– *'Most of your heroines are divorced or widowed, and those who
are still married are not living happily'.*
'I do not believe there is harmony in married life. I have known
marriages that I thought were happy but I found out they were not.
I see more and more unsuccessful, fragile bonds. I write about things
that the whole Ultra-Orthodox world knows to exist, but keeps
secret. I know of a young woman whose husband abused her and

she climbed to the top of a building and jumped off with her three-year-old daughter. He of course remarried, but she, poor thing, and her child, paid with their lives. I am torn over conjugal issues. I disapprove of adultery: but is it preferable to live with a man you do not love? And a child that sees no love at home, what kind of married life will he have? With my sensitive radar, I detect the façades, and dissolve them. My society considers it a sin to bring it out in the open, and I hope I shall not be doomed to eternal hell for writing about it. My children have read my stories and reassured me that the devil is not as black as he's painted'.

– *'Your stories portray a multitude of sick, handicapped and distorted characters. Illness is almost the natural state of existence'.* 'A lack of harmony – and this is the bitter reality – creates deficiency, a constant, hopeless search for fulfillment, and it results in sick, distorted characters'.

Loveless mothers are a recurrent motif in Bat Shahar's stories. Her mother was the spoilt child of rich parents and was accustomed to fine clothes, card-playing and reading women's magazines. 'All her life she was weak and childish, a dependent woman who wasted her time on trivialities and had no understanding of money', says Bat-Shahar:

> The cold mothers in my stories, who cannot give love, are derived from my own childhood. I never had a real mother. When my children complain that I am egotistical, I tell them they're right: if a person had no model of motherhood, he can do no better himself.

She always felt emotionally sterile, lacking knowledge of love. Physical contact is difficult for her:

> My children would like a Mom, to cry on her bosom, but I'm not like that. When my conscience troubles me I send my married daughter Gefilte Fish I have made, to compensate for the fact that I cannot give her the support she wants, or look after her small children. I have my own concerns – studies, reading, writing – and they are very important to me. I'm critical of my children; it's hard for me to accept weakness, especially from my daughter. I'm a feminist, and I think a woman has to be very strong.

Some years ago, motivated by some obscure need, she went to work in an old people's home. For two years this delicate woman fed them, washed them, changed their soiled diapers, emptied their bedpans:

> Only later did I realize that in looking after these helpless old people, I was seeking a father and a mother. By exhausting myself with strangers, I wanted to atone, to make it up to my parents for the love I never gave them, and to myself for the love I never received from them. Of course, it didn't work.

Out of that experience, she wrote the story, *The Butterfly Dance*. She startles me when she suddenly asks:

> Have you seen Antonioni's film *The Red Desert*? The heroine is running with a child in her arms, and sees a labourer eating a sandwich. She asks him where he bought it. He points towards a kiosk. 'Sell me your sandwich', she implores him and gives him money, even though the sandwich has already been nibbled. She runs off to some hiding-place and obsessively swallows the food. Clearly it is not hunger for bread that is driving her, but an emotional hunger: the husband who does not love her, and the lover who does not show her enough affection, and the lack of meaning in her life. When I saw the film I knew that – even though my way of life is so different from hers – that was me: I too am driven by emotional hunger.

– *'I'm surprised that you go to the cinema'*.
'It is forbidden in my society, and we are not allowed to have a television at home, but I took a university course on literature and film, so I had a chance to see all the masterpieces'.

She frequently writes of attraction between women:

> I don't think eroticism is my forte. For me love begins in the head, not under the belt. I am not a lesbian, though for years I thought I might be. I was attracted to women more than to men. Both because a woman is less threatening and because there is a certain softness that only a woman can give, an intimacy that asks nothing in return. There is no religious prohibition against friendship between women. For me a strange man constitutes a

far greater threat, a danger that the family nest may crumble and disintegrate. It is a taboo that I have to guard against and it is not easy, not at all easy'.

*– 'Do you regret being born where you were born? Would you enjoy the freedom of secular, liberal life?'*
'No. I had to be born where I was born, and live through my perplexities. I cannot erase the Ultra-Orthodox world from my consciousness, nor can I erase literature and what it has given me. The conflict between the two worlds makes me what I am. I believe in God, I strictly observe all the rituals and commandments, I have no thoughts of apostasy, and I believe with all my heart that there is an eye that sees and an ear that hears and that all one's deeds are written down in the book of life. I could not live in a world without meaning; if it were not for my faith in God, and for my stolen hours of writing, I would kill myself'.


TRANSLATED INTO ENGLISH

Bat-Shahar, H., 'Between the Geranium Pots' [*Bein Aztizei Hageranium*; found in *Calling the Bats*], in R. Domb (ed.), *New Women's Writings from Israel* (London: Vallentine Mitchell, 1996).

# CHAPTER FOURTEEN

# Yona Wallach
## (1944–85)

# Never Shall I Hear God's Sweet Voice

In 1983, a year and a half after it was published in the literary magazine, *Eton 77*, Miriam Ta'asa-Glazer, the deputy Education Minister, learned about 'Tefillin', a poem by Yona Wallach. The iconoclastic poet, the most eccentric and colourful that Israeli literature ever knew, described a sexual encounter, in which the woman asks her lover to tie her up with tefillin: the Phylacteries that Jewish men are required to bind on their arms and head during each weekday Morning Prayer, two small sacred black boxes with long leather straps attached to them.

> Rub them hard against me/ stimulate me everywhere/make me swoon with sensation/move them over my clitoris/tie my waist with them/ so I'll come quickly.

The deputy Education Minister had not seen the poem, only read about it, but stated that the poet is 'a deranged person ... a beast in heat that writes such a poem, and publishes it ... it's anarchy'. In the midst of the public dispute that followed, the Israeli Writers' Organization filed a complaint about the term 'a beast in heat', and even the Israeli Parliament was involved. Although wrestling with a deadly cancer that was soon to defeat her, Yona Wallach did not wink at the scandal. It was quite in line with her extravagant personality, as the woman who transformed Israeli poetry, and introduced a different kind of language, as well as sexual ambiguity, feminism and gender issues.

'Wallach adopts males' pornographic language in order to protest against woman's oppression', explains Dr Rachel Giora of the Tel Aviv University:

> The speaker in 'Tefillin' is acting out her anger with pornography. She asks her lover-abuser to, 'ride me, I'm a mare/ pull my head back/ till I scream with pain', but at the end of the poem, she strangles her abuser by taking the ritual ropes used by men in prayers that exclude women: 'I'll wind them several times around your neck, on one side/and on the other I'll tie them to something solid/especially heavy maybe twisting/I'll pull and I'll pull/till your soul leaves you/till I choke you /completely with the tefillin'. Using irony that was so subtle that it often eluded her readers and critics, Wallach dissociated herself from the language and practice of oppressive pornography.

She was born in the village of Kiryat Ono, near Tel Aviv, in the summer of 1944, a second daughter to Esther and Michael Wallach, and was named Yona, after three dead relatives who had borne that name: her father's mother, a niece, and an uncle. She thus began her life with a burden of doom and androgyny.

She was just four years old when her father was killed in the War of Independence, his body tortured and mutilated. He had been among the founders of Kiryat Ono, and the street where his widow and two daughters continued to live was named after the dead hero. For most of her life, she lived in the family home, as if unable to uproot herself from Michael Wallach Street.

'I did not have a male role model, I needed to bake it and make it from all sorts of men that I knew', Wallach said years later in an interview given to Hilit Yeshurun, the editor of *Chadarim* [Rooms] literary magazine. 'I became my own father. I wore masculine clothes and took responsibility'.

She was a precocious child, repeatedly watching the films that were screened in the local cinema which her mother had leased after she was left widowed, adding this evening job to her daily work as a school secretary. Yona developed a cinematic approach, and the poems she wrote later were picturesque, often like scenes from movies, or video clips that preceded their time.

Yona always aspired to be a writer, confiding to a friend that she dreamed of writing a novel like *War and Peace*. She was a vivacious, rebellious teenager, wearing blue jeans with her father's shirts that were still kept in the closet a decade after his death. At 16, she had her first abortion. Because of her behaviour she was thrown out of Tichon Chadash, a prestigious high school in Tel Aviv. The head-mistress – who acknowledged extraordinary talents among her students, such as those of pianist Daniel Barenboim, allowing him go off to rehearsals and performances on school days – did not spot any uniqueness in the 14-year-old Yona, and complained that she was neglecting her studies and passing the time doodling in her notebooks and scribbling poems.

Wallach was better integrated into the Avni Art School, the bohemian atmosphere allowing her eccentricity to blossom. She was not only immersed in art; this was the beginning of her lifelong experimentation with life-styles: drugs, diverse sexuality and states of awareness. 'Aged 18, when her friends were all drafted into the obligatory army service, Yona stepped into the recruiting office and declared that she, the war-orphan of Michael Wallach, would not serve in the army', writes biographer Yigal Sarna. 'That summer, she approached the Eked publishing house, which was renowned for nurturing young poets. She was deeply offended when they refused to publish her'. Back at home she had an hallucination; her unisex name, Yona, meaning 'dove' (and also the name of a male biblical prophet), was confused in her blazing mind with Yonatan, the protagonist of a popular nursery rhyme, and with Yehonatan, King Saul's son and the soul mate and possible lover of the young King David.

> I'm running on the bridge/ and the kids after me/Yonatan/Yonatan they call/a bit of blood/just a bit of blood to wipe off the honey. / I agree to the prick of a thumbtack ... /but the kids want/and they're kids/ and I'm Yonatan ...

At the end of this poem of sexual abuse, Yonatan is beheaded with gladioli, sword-like flowers, and the severed head continues to talk to its torturers, even forgiving them. 'The protagonist of the poem reminds us of Jesus Christ, not only because of his persecution by the crowd, but also because of the prick of the nail, that intuitively connects to the crucifixion wounds', explains Dr Lily Rattok of the Tel Aviv University, in *Angel of Fire*, her study of

Wallach's poetry:

> Yonatan can also be perceived as a feminine figure, hunted down by a group of men, who do not hide their intentions. The victim's consent to a prick of a thumbtack, with the connotation of violent penetration, stimulates their appetite, and they are no longer content with just a bit of blood to wipe off the honey. The two interpretations, the Christian and the Feminist, leave no doubt that Wallach identifies with the victim.

In her interview with Hilit Yeshurun in 1984, a year before her death, Wallach made her identification with Jesus Christ even more transparent.

> I would hear [God's] voice from a young age. I loved Him awfully. From the time I was a small child He would call me. Once in the garden, I was a sleepwalking child, I saw a cloud of fog in which I became immersed, and then I went home. And all these years there has been a voice that has called me through sleep, 'Yona, Yona, Yona'. All the years I think He wished to support me. I think He wished to look at me, and then He came closer. Only later He shouted: 'Why didn't you call me, I would have come' ... There was Jesus, and after Jesus Yona had to come along. God wants to appear again on the stage of history.

Her cosmic mission, so she perceived it, was to be achieved through poetry, the creative artist being the new figure of the Messiah.

Yona was celebrating her own sexuality with men and women alike, and she often stole her boyfriends' girlfriends. To a girlfriend on the eve of her marriage, she boldly said, 'Does your chin quiver when you're with him?' In 1963, the 19-year-old Yona found herself pregnant again, possibly by any one of a number of men she was sleeping with. Her several abortions – and she had undergone at least four - were not just a result of the pre-pill days, but also, as she explained, an attempt to explore motherhood without having to be a mother.

Not long after, using the metaphor of the biblical Absalom, the beloved son of King David, who died when his long beautiful hair was caught in the bushes and strangled him, Wallach wrote a poem by that name:

I must once again/be reminded of my son Absalom/ whose hair was caught in my womb/and I couldn't/complete Absalom my son ... /how my stomach is empty from Absalom my son ...

She was living at her mother's home, going to art school and frequenting cafés where artists and poets used to sit together, dramatic, with her long hair, fair skin, high boots and extraordinary clothes. To support herself, she worked as a nursery teacher's assistant, telling the enchanted three year olds tales about dragons and kings. Five months later, she dropped out. It was her first and last steady job. Many of her poems imitate the singsong of nursery rhymes, their brash violence or sexuality contrasting with the quasi-innocence of the children's songs.

Wallach belonged to the 'Tel Aviv Poets', a group headed by Meir Weiseltier and Yair Hurvitz, which emerged in the 1960s and was influenced by American Beat Poetry. The three of them became friends and lovers, sharing not only a poetic vision, but also a painful biography, all of them having been fatherless as young children.

The first signs of Yona Wallach's mental breakdown came at 18, after watching Marguerite Duras and Alain Rene's *Hiroshima Mon Amour* and having visions of her father's death. She was first treated at 20, after manifesting impulses to murder her mother. A year later she consented to be hospitalised in a mental institute in Jerusalem. To the psychiatrist, she said that she was admitting herself in order to understand herself better, and was looking forward to a pleasant experience. She was given a room of her own, and the permission to write and create, a rare privilege in that place.

'She calls herself homosexual, although she does not rule out relationships with men', biographer Yigal Sarna quotes from the medical records of Professor Marcel Asahel, Wallach's therapist. She reported having hallucinations, seeing severed heads, and was given LSD, which in 1965 was still considered a promising treatment. 'She sometimes tries to seduce younger patients, or those weaker then her', Professor Asahel noted in a report. 'She forces sexual relations on them, without their co-operation'. Four months later, she was released, no better than upon her admittance. Staying in a rented room in Jerusalem, she continued hallucinating severed heads and mutilated bodies like her father's.

Her poems from that time were published first in literary supplements and magazines, and then in 1966 in her first book,

*Things*. In this, the libido is the heroine's own doom, pulling her towards the dangers of sexuality, and making her an easy prey. Wallach portrayed a number of manifestations of that conflict, through the different personas of her poems, both male and female, most of them bearing foreign names. Theresa, from a poem of that name, carefully welded her mouth shut so that nothing would penetrate it. Lotte 'takes pills against different/feelings of mystery'. Cecilia 'finished all the chocolates/and wiped her mouth carefully/so the ants wouldn't come'. Christina is a small girl who falls prey to a group of boys who gang rape her and turn her into 'the Christina', a female-Christ, and a sexual object with no personal identity. Wallach's book was ecstatically received.

At that time, she was involved in a sado-masochistic relationship with Tadeush, the man she was about to marry, but she recoiled just before taking the vows. Only in 1983, in her book *Wild Light*, did some of the more blatant poems written under the inspiration of the sexual practices and fantasies she shared with Tadeush, become published: 'Strawberries', 'Tefillin', and others.

Wallach was attracted to homosexual men, and many of them became her intimate lovers. 'I compensated myself by a special talent to change sexes', she said in an interview.

> I was never enough woman; I've always been half boy. I had to dress like a boy, be a boy ... I needed to identify with something stronger than I was in my feminine environment. Like all women I learned to hate women, to hate weakness and love men, be half a boy, and it ruined my life ... One should remain a woman and not deny what you are, not be half a cock.

In her later poems, she found the solution: a woman can bring back sensuality and humanity into the universe, by connecting man into his lost vitality: 'I'll be your Id', she said in one of her poems.

Professor Miri Kubovy of Harvard University views Wallach as a pioneer of Israeli feminism and post-modernism. Kubovy believes that Wallach is:

> ... the most cosmopolitan artist that Israel ever produced – without ever having gone out of the country. She preceded her time in her intuitions, with no terminology, in understanding and phrasing cultural, social and political processes.

But, living her life and 'crossing the world like a live torch, like a man on fire', as Hilit Yeshurun, her posthumous editor described her, took its toll. Wallach exhibited paranoid behaviour, accusing her formerly best friends of stealing her books from her head. She used to phone literary editors, screaming that they were not to publish this or that poet who was robbing her.

In 1974 she made a serious suicide attempt, but refused to be hospitalised. All that time, she was publishing her poems and received three literary prizes, but was living on the support of her mother, since she herself did not work. Two musicians, who became her friends and lovers, wrote tunes to her poems, the three of them establishing a rock group. They performed in clubs, Yona wearing high boots and tight clothes on stage, shocking and exciting her audiences reading in her husky voice poems like 'Strawberries', a male sexual fantasy in which the woman is asked to hold a bowl of strawberries while wearing nothing under her dress, 'and afterwards/strings will lift you up/invisible or visible/and lower you/directly on my prick'. One of their songs, resembling a nursery rhyme, about a girl sleeping with her soft teddy bear, was picked to be included in a children's song contest. Wallach altered two words in that masturbation poem, originally titled 'Gogol's Puppet', turning it into 'Go to Sleep, Teddybear', fooling not only the judging audience as to the original meaning, but also winning the first prize.

It is amazing that Wallach, the most sexually unabashed woman poet in Hebrew literature, identified with Rachel. That romantic, melancholic poet came as a pioneer from Russia to Palestine and died in 1931, deserted – on account of the deadly tuberculosis that plagued her – by all her high-profile lovers, leaders of the newly established Jewish community. 'Wallach believed that she was the reincarnation of Rachel', says Dr Lily Rattok:

> She kept it as a secret, but travelled several times to Rachel's tomb near the Sea of Galilee. She told a friend, 'When I were Rachel, I was a coward and nice to the guys, but now that I have come back to life, and not for many years, I intend to write about everything'.

Aged 41, just like Rachel at her death, Yona Wallach died in agony from her own fatal illness. She described the 12-year gap between Rachel's death and her own birth as the life of 'a street cat'.

Dr Rattok believes that the choice by the wild and revolutionary Wallach, of the humble, timid Rachel, is extraordinary, because of the contrast between them. It seems that Wallach read between the lines of Rachel, and sensed that Rachel formerly had a free spirit, which was squashed by the male world. Through Rachel, Wallach realized how dear is the price a woman pays if she accepts the brainwashing of patriarchy. Several of Wallach's poems, including 'Yonatan', converse with Rachel's poems on the same theme. 'Wallach expanded the scope of Hebrew women's poetry, in terms of subject matter and language', explains Dr Rattok:

> She used strong, blunt language describing sex, to break taboos. She adopted the language of pornography to protest against the patriarchal culture, that sees woman as a sexual object. She combines the two traditions in Hebrew literature: male and female. She achieved her poetic triumphs because she not only was influenced by her male colleagues, like Zach, Avidan, Weiseltier and Hurvitz, but also by female poets like Rachel, Leah Goldberg and Dalia Ravikovitch.

Yona was living with her mother, who had Parkinson's disease; her ambivalence towards her mother making their relationship a hell. In the medical records, there were hints that the bruises that Esther Wallach suffered were made by her daughter's hand. In 1981, the 36-year-old Wallach discovered a lump in her breast, but refused to have a biopsy. 'Every incision seemed to her like a mutilation or a beheading, she was afraid of a treatment that might take off her skin, invade her body and make her bleed endlessly', biographer Sarna writes.

> She put off the medical examination for almost two years, and when she did, there were already metastasis in her bones. She died on 26 September 1985. 'I want to go home, to father', were her last words before sinking into unconsciousness.

## TRANSLATIONS INTO ENGLISH

Wallach, Y., *Selected Poems* [trans. L. Zisquit] (New York: Sheep Meadow Press, 1997).

# CHAPTER FIFTEEN

# Meir Shalev
## (1948– )

# The Emasculated Man and the Queen Bee

'Human traits are not content with the set routes paved by here-dity', wrote novelist Meir Shalev. 'They also pass on in mother's milk, in bedtime stories, in the touch of fingertips, and in the drip-ping saliva of a kiss'.

Through mother's milk and saliva, Meir absorbed stories from his parents, Izhak and Batia Shalev. Aged only three and a half, they taught him to read, and at five, he delved into his first novel, *Don Quixote* by Cervantes, 'and even before that, I browsed in a diction-ary. From infancy, I was a man of words'.

He was born in 1948 into the War of Independence, in the mythological village of Nahalal, to a distinguished pioneering clan. In his first 12 years his parents shuttled between his birth-village in the Valley of Jezreel, and Jerusalem, where they finally settled down. His father, a poet and novelist, would take him every Shabbat on hikes, walking for 15 or 20 miles, using the Old Testament as their tour guide to follow in the footsteps of the Patriarchs. From the time Meir turned 13, he would go to Nahalal during the summer vacations, to strengthen his frail muscles on the farm of his maternal uncles. 'My shortsightedness pushed me into the arms of memory and reading', he wrote in his novel *Esau*. 'There, among the pages, I discovered the lucid people, the explicable twists and turns, the horizon that never fades'.

He was one of those kids that wrench a special permission from the librarian to borrow two books a day. 'If every boy became friends with a librarian, a natural-science teacher and a tall, forgiving woman, the world would be a different place', Yechiel Abramson, the village librarian, tells the bespectacled child-protagonist of *Esau*. Meir Shalev himself befriended a librarian, and remembers his nature teacher affectionately:

> Although I never had any tall, forgiving woman; probably because I'm not tall enough. A miserable childhood and an adventurous manhood is the gold mine of a writer, but my own life has been uneventful and banal. I never had the life of Primo Levi, Hemingway or Jack London, that have only to leaf through their private diary to produce a novel. I like literature to be larger than life, so I make up a life'.

*Esau* is the story of a clan, from 1920 to the present, narrated by one of its sons, Esau, the writer, a confirmed bachelor and a Don Juan. His mother is Sarah, descended from a line of Russian converts, and his father is Avram the baker, from an ancient Sepharadi family. In spite of the Modern Hebrew and the current setting, the story has a biblical flavour, hinted at by the names of the Patriarchs that Shalev has given his protagonists. 'I read the Bible just as other people read psychology or literature', Shalev says:

> All my novels bear a deep influence of the Scriptures; my favourite biblical protagonist is Jacob. His life reads like Ingmar Bergman's *Pictures of a Marriage*, a real, earthy life: he sleeps with his wives; inseminates his cattle; and sires offspring. He's the true father of Israel. He stole the seniority from his twin-brother Esau, but in the long run, it's not clear who got the better deal. The biblical Jacob summed up his life with a terrible epitaph: 'The days of my life were short and bad'. He defined his life as a failure.

The fictional Jacob of Shalev's novel, steals the heart of Leah, who is Esau's love, and marries her. The disappointed Esau leaves the family bakery to his brother, and immigrates to the USA. But, shortly after Jacob and Leah's marriage, they begin to drift apart. Then, following the death of their soldier son Benjamin, Leah cuddles up in her dead son's bed, and falls into an unending sleep. When Jacob can't bear his longings for his son any more, he beds his dormant wife, and she bears him a young son, to be his comfort. His twin brother, the writer Esau, has in the meantime achieved fame and fortune in America. *The Bread Book* that he writes becomes a bestseller. 'Like my father and my brother I also make my living out of bread, but I do not bake it any more, I only write about it', Esau boasts. 'I unloaded the burden of family suffering, the inferno of the stove and the blaze of the moulds'.

Although Shalev's novel bears the title *Esau*, Jacob is the real protagonist, and his story is told through the eyes of his twin. Which brother knows more about life: the eloquent, well-read one, who had several women, or the one who experienced life in the simple, tortured way, and cannot express it in words?

> In one of his novels, my father wrote that the nerves of memory are intertwined with the nerves of smell. I too diagnose the seasons by the smell of the air, the earth, the sand, a smell of crashed grass or reaped clover.

Says Meir Shalev:

> During my army service, one freezing winter night in the Galilee, we were navigating through the hills and suddenly were bewitched by the smell of bread. The smell was our compass, and it guided us through the darkness until we arrived at a bakery. It was two hours past midnight, we knocked on the window; the baker wiped the mist from the glass, and saw three miserable, dripping-wet soldiers. He gave each of us a hot Challa bread straight from the pan, and a cup of coffee, and sent us on our way. I do not remember a greater happiness in my life, eating bread which was home, care, life itself.

When Shalev was a student of psychology at the Hebrew University, he supported himself by doing night shifts as an ambulance driver:

> Throughout the night, the smell from 'Angel's Bakery' enveloped the city. The place would attract night-refugees, each with his pain, sitting in the bakery antechamber and chewing their bread. I knew that when I wrote a novel, my protagonist would be a man who does a basic job. I'm not interested in writing about insurance agents and accountants and computer programmers, I prefer farmers, mechanics or bakers.

Shalev's decision to study psychology was motivated by a wish
to specialize in animal behaviour, and especially insects that were,
and still are, his passion: from childhood, he filled his parents home
with spider traps. However, he did not enjoy the academic experience and cut his studies short to become a television reporter. He
has been writing all his adult life, but being a strict critic, he has
destroyed everything, including 100 pages of a utopian novel,
which described the imaginary materialization of Herzl's idea to
establish a Jewish state in Uganda. He gave himself a deadline, to
publish a novel before turning 40, and after 14 years of television
journalism, he took a year off to fulfill his dream. After 16 full
drafts, he finally let go of *The Blue Mountain*. It did not fail, was a
huge success, and since it's publication in 1988 has sold hundreds of
thousands copies and turned Meir Shalev into a full-time writer.

In an era when young mavericks in their early twenties storm
and conquer the bestseller chart, Shalev sounds almost apologetic
that he was such a late bloomer. 'I needed the maturity, crystalliza-
tion and patience of age, to be able to write a novel'. But if he could
begin his life all over again, he would prefer to be a scientist,
specializing in the natural sciences. He applies the same approach to
literature, and for the research of *Esau* he filled 400 pages in his
notebooks. For six months he interviewed old Jerusalemites about
life under the British Mandate, and collected testimonies about the
earthquake which shook the city on 12 July 1927, the day his
protagonist Sarah takes her twin sons and her husband in the
chariot of the Archbishop and flees to a village in the Sharon. Shalev
spent many nights in bakeries, chatting with bakers and their sons,
and when he wrote about a butcher in *Four Meals*, he became
apprenticed in a butcher's shop, learning how to cut up a cow:

> I am not faint-hearted; I love things that are made of flesh and
> blood. The real difficulty is to describe each character from his
> or her own consciousness, and not from my own. For example,
> Jacob's maxims about life must be those that suit a simple
> person, matching his own experiences that he acquired in 'the
> university of life', and should be not too deep, nor too shallow.
> I have some firsthand knowledge of grief, as cousins of mine
> were killed in wars, but I decided to interview bereaved parents,
> to describe faithfully the grief of Jacob and Leah for their soldier
> son Benjamin. I wanted to make sure that every phrase I wrote
> would be authentic, something I heard with my own ears, and

not invented. For example, the mutual blame between Jacob and Leah, why did Benjamin volunteer to a combat unit? Or the scene at the graveside during the funeral, when Jacob looks at the flat tummies of the girls who were his son's lovers, wondering if any of them is pregnant, and decides to make another son for himself.

– *'Benjamin was killed as a result of "friendly fire", by our own troops, in 1967. During your army service, you were involved in an identical event'.*
'True. Two army units mistakenly opened fire at each other in November 1967 in the Jordan Valley. Four of my friends were killed, and four others and I were wounded. Senior army officers besieged my hospital bed and threatened me that I was not to divulge a word about the circumstances of the mishap. I asked what I should do if the bereaved parents came to inquire. They said, "Tell them that it's a military secret". I refused to withhold the truth. A few days later a father came from a kibbutz, his son was an officer, and was killed next to me. He sat weeping by my bed and demanded that I reconstruct that night. I did, and he thanked me deeply. My own serious injuries hurt me less than the encounter with that father, who died of grief some years later'.

Pain is a recurrent theme with Shalev, based upon his own experience, and also on those of his brother-in-law, who is a physician in a pain clinic in the Hadassah hospital in Jerusalem. Shalev sat at the clinic with the consent of the patients, and made notes:

Pain, like love, is the most common feeling, but the most dividing one. When an Eskimo is in pain, his moans sound exactly the same as those of an Australian, but if one needs to describe pain in words, it's impossible to convey the feeling to another person. I noticed that the first thing a patient does when he has to give his doctor a verbal description of pain, is to look for a metaphor: 'It hurts like a hammer in the stomach … like white smoke scorching flesh', or, 'It's the same feeling while you make love, but it's in the back'. The Pain Doctor in my book says, 'Pain turns them into poets'.

Shalev writes in layers – not in linear order – episodes that will eventually build up a coherent plot:

There's an image of a writer, sitting in a dusky room with empty wine bottles and cups of coffee, and the Muses hovering over his head. It's nonsense. There are many technical sides to writing, and I see myself as a craftsman, who wants to produce a good, polished product. I write like a baker, sweating and tormenting against the oven and doing the work with absolute perseverance.

When he's writing, he says, he lives with two families: the one in his novel, and his own. He gets up at seven, and if his wife, who is an airhostess, is abroad, he organizes the house and the children, and then goes downtown to an office to write. At 13:00, just like a labourer who switches off his lathe for a lunch break; he shuts down the computer and returns home to prepare lunch. He considers himself a fairly good housewife, is proud of his skills in cleaning and cooking, and prefers simple food: chicken soup, mashed potatoes and steak:

My reading taste is the same: unsophisticated books; ones that do not try to show off. I do not read books when I write, as they distract me, but I cannot fall asleep without leafing through some pages, so I take books that I'm already familiar with. Writing creates much adrenalin; I'm so excited that I cannot sleep. Sometimes I begin writing at four in the morning, and I walk a lot, or drive around in my jeep, to calm myself down.

Contrary to those who are enamoured with every word they put on paper, Shalev is quick to throw away:

It's like a basket of apples, if one of them is rotten, it should be thrown away or else it will contaminate the others. I constantly fear that any moment, my motorcycle will turn over and I'll be killed, and my notes and drafts will be left for all to see and publish. I'm not going to give anyone this pleasure.

His male protagonists have the physical build of strong men: a farmer, a baker, a stonecutter or a butcher, but deep inside they are feeble, inarticulate, almost emasculated, in contrast to the heroines who are dominant Queen Bees with a mythological quality about them. Raphael, the butcher from *In His House in the Wilderness*, is raised by his mother, sister, grandmother and aunts – five castrating women who, even at his ripe age of 52, still boss him around. His only way out is to flee to the desert, and live there on his own. The pressure-cooker of the close-knit family touches on the verge of sibling and parent–child incest, which is a recurrent theme with Shalev. The long parade of beauties that march in and out of Esau's bedroom all resemble his mother, like 'a duckling following the first creature that he saw when he emerged from his egg'. Rabinovitz, the farmer from *As A Few Days*, is similarly described as attracted to his wife because she and his sister were like two peas in a pod. Wanting to compliment her, he says, 'You are my sister'.

– '*The mother in* Esau *is ever-present; all her son's loves are in her likeness. She even resembles your own mother*'.
'I do not deny it, although their beauty is of a different kind. Sarah is blonde and robust, and my mother was petite and dark and, unlike Sarah, who was an uneducated peasant, mother was a high school teacher of literature and the Bible. But you're right; both are strong women, very close to their sons, with a deep integrity. My mother read the first drafts of the book, and was touched by Sarah's character. She certainly noticed the similarity between them. When I wrote that Sarah dies of a fatal cancer, I had no idea this would be my mother's fate. It just suited a strong woman, who had no ache in her life that the only thing that could kill her was an illness that grew out of her own tissues. I was in the middle of writing when my mother was suddenly diagnosed with a violent cancer. My sister Raphaela was alarmed, and asked me to omit the cancer and the death of the heroine from the book, because of the bad omen, but mother, in her integrity, requested that I should not change anything'.

Shalev wrote the last 100 pages of the book frantically, racing against time. He wanted his mother to hold the book in her hand. 'It was a joint mission of both, but we didn't make it. She died before I finished, and I dedicated the book to her'.
*Esau* is about love, and Shalev feels that as much as one speaks or writes about the subject, one doesn't understand it any better:

Everything that there is to say about love has already been written in the Bible or in Greek mythology. Every uttering becomes a cliché, a mediocre manual for the preservation of marriage. I aim to tell a story and not to dictate maxims. I understand the protagonists I created quite well, much better than I understand myself, but I cannot deduce from their own loves and loses, to my own private life.

Like Raphael who wanders into the wilderness, Meir Shalev expresses his suffocation and frustration at the current face of Israel, by frequent jeep trips to the mountains or to the desert:

> Jerusalem has become an unbearable city, with so much violence and madness. It's a town to visit, yearn for, but not to live in. Jerusalem is the greatest proof that love should not be materialized, that the realization of a dream, corrupts and brutalizes.

After a devastating earthquake in Armenia in the early 1990s, Shalev read a newspaper report about a woman who was buried with her baby for several days among the rubble, and stabbed her finger and let her baby drink her own blood. A few days later they were rescued, fatigued but alive. He filed the clipping for future use, thinking that the scene was more incredible than he could have ever invented:

> Life is more fantastic than literature. If you read a novel about a man who was walking along in the street and a woman dropped on him from the second floor, and they fell in love and got married, you'd say it's a bag of bullshit. But if you read it in a newspaper, you'd say 'How sweet'. One demands literature to behave more logically than life. The inner logic of my stories is not always discernable; it's like a puzzle, a subterranean map that has to be excavated. The thin border between truth and falsity does not cease to intrigue me.

## TRANSLATIONS INTO ENGLISH

Shalev, M., *The Blue Mountain* [*Roman Russi*; trans. H. Halkin] (New York: Harper Collins, 1991).
—— *Esau* [trans. B. Harshav] (New York: Harper Collins, 1994).
—— *The Loves of Judith* [*Keyamin Achadim*; trans. B. Harshav] (New York: Ecco Press, 1999).
—— *Four Meals* [*Keyamin Achadim*; trans. B. Harshav] (Edinburgh: Canongate, 2000).

# CHAPTER SIXTEEN

# David Grossman
## (1954– )

# *I'm an Egg without a Shell*

In the corner of the small balcony in the Grossmans' home in Jerusalem, rested a tall-legged shabby old armchair. For days on end, the red-headed, thin, bespectacled six-year-old David would hide beneath it and tell himself stories, things that he wished would happen to him:

> If a good fairy had come to me then, and told me that some day, people will read these stories and they will be translated into foreign languages, I would say that the fairy had gone nutty. I was a desperate child, I felt that no one understood me; no one wanted to listen to me; and that there was no place for someone like me in the world. One has to fight to have his voice heard in the amplified deafening hum of family and society. If you are desperate enough, at the end you'll break the walls surrounding you.

He was a wunderkind, and began school at five. Aged nine, he enrolled in a radio quiz for adults about the life and work of the Yiddish humourist Shalom Aleichem. The prize was 1,110 Israeli pounds (several months' salary).

> I sat through the qualifying exams with all sorts of experts and university academics, and made it. But the General Director of

the radio said it was immoral that such a young child would set
out to win so much money, so they made a compromise and let
me in the studio during the competition, on condition that only
if the contesters would not know an answer, would I be allowed
to give one. And I did, and my voice was heard. Then I was
offered the chance to be a child-reporter on a radio youth
programme, and I travelled the country and interviewed the
President and many famous writers.

He was ten years old when he wrote his first story, *Gill Runs off
to the Circus*, sharing a typewriter with his mother, who at night
typed student assignments to help support the family.

David Grossman read philosophy and theatre at the Hebrew
University. His first children's book, *Duel*, was published in late
1982, and a few weeks later, his first adult novel, *Runner*, came out.
Since then he has developed a parallel career, zigzagging between
the two readerships. Children are the protagonists of his adult
novels, and grown-ups enjoy reading his novels for youth.
Grossman believes that in order to know oneself, one must know
one's own parents. 'As a child, I wondered what did I inherit from
my parents, and today I'm asking myself what part of me is in my
children. That's the issue explored in all my books'.

When Grossman published his *See Under: Love* in 1986,
Professor George Steiner described the first part as 'One of the
greatest achievements in modern novel'. In it, Grossman explores
the gradual awareness of the Holocaust, and the slaughter of the six
million, as perceived by an Israeli boy in the 1960s. It is based on
David's own growing awareness during the Eichmann trial in
Jerusalem; as his own father emigrated in 1936 from Galicia, a
world that was devoured some years later in the flames that
consumed the Jews of Europe. The second part of the novel
portrays the story of one person out of the six million: Bruno
Schulz, an unknown Jewish writer who was shot to death for no
reason by an SS officer. Grossman's novel saved Schultz from oblivion, and new editions of his works were published all over the
world.

Grossman went on and ventured into the nightmares of childhood in the emerging Israel through Aharon Kleinfeld, the protagonist of *The Book of Intimate Grammar*. It was a society of
displaced people, who had survived a huge catastrophe and were

trying with all their might to build a new life. They clung to food and to their meager possessions, creating a concrete arbitrary world, which corrupted language and trampled Aharon's sensitive, child-artist soul.

Grossman struggled with his childhood memories, reliving painful aspects of himself: a small, thin, restless boy, always on the alert, nervous as an old man, fighting for his life:

> The book took me to the verge of losing the ability to live a bearable life. When you write a novel, you must deconstruct yourself pitilessly, and disarm yourself from the defense mechanisms you labouriously built for so many years. From novel to novel, the defense filters that guard my emotions disappear, I become exposed and vulnerable. Unlike the common misconception that writing frees you from your demons and helps you solve your problems, my books have only rephrased my problems more acutely.

In all his novels, Grossman deals with the arbitrariness of an external force that brutally invades the life of a person. In *See Under: Love*, this force is Nazism. In *The Yellow Wind* and *The Smile of the Lamb*, the force is Israeli military occupation. In *The Book of Intimate Grammar*, it is the invasion of external norms and clichés into the life of a sensitive person; a portrait of an artist as a young man.

In 1991, after finishing *The Book of Intimate Grammar*, he decided to take a year off from writing and experience ordinary life, but the first thing he did was to write a documentary book, *Sleeping on a Wire* – conversations with Israeli Arabs. Then he stopped writing altogether, frequented the cinema with his wife, entertained, travelled abroad. And when the year was over, he began to breathe differently, and to create a world of sweet illusion, that the writer and the reader would not want to wake from. After the brutality of his previous books, he needed one with a happy ending, and with love and wishes coming true, with the comfort of fantasy:

> I wanted to connect to my happier and freer parts, and I created Nono, the protagonist of *The Zigzag Kid*. He is my other self: optimist, active, wild; a child-actor, changing roles constantly; a child who wishes to enchant, and has something of the crook or the charlatan about him. I did many of the pranks that Nono

does in the book: ate a beetle to impress a girl; walked on the edge of the roof of a three-storey house; crawled inside the sewage; climbed on cranes in building sites. Things I'm reluctant to elaborate on, lest my children should learn from me.

In *The Zigzag Kid*, an adult fairytale, Grossman toys around with several well-known literary and film motifs: the Charming Crook, the Frog-Prince, the widower marrying the governess of his children as in *The Sound of Music*, the Sad Princess, the Swan's Song, the Happy Orphan, the Lonely Avenger, Alladin's Jin. Thirteen-year-old Amnon (Nono) Feuerberg loses his wild-spirited mother, Zohara, in mysterious circumstances before he has turned one year old. His father Jacob, a dry, reticent police officer, has involved himself since the death of his wife in an unrelenting struggle against crime. The mother figure in the story is Gabi, a spinster of 40, clever and charming, who, unfortunately, like the Frog-Prince, was cursed with an ugly face and an obese shapeless body, that only love can save her from. As the father's personal assistant in the police station, she's in love with him, and has been parenting his son with immense dedication. But, refusing to recover from his wife's death, he turns down Gabi's frequent marriage proposals. Nono loves Gabi, and serves as a makeshift matchmaker. 'Love is the activating force of the story. It's fun to write about a love that turns out well. In life, it seldom happens'.

Grossman, who has been a child radio-actor, acquired the habit of testing texts by reading them aloud:

> My greatest pleasure in writing the book were the five weeks in which the kids would come to our bed every evening. I read them *The Zigzag Kid*, and received the most unabashed criticism, as never before. When they fidgeted, or began to kick and pinch each other, or jump on me and strangle me, I got the message and struck out the whole passage. One protagonist had an ugly birthmark on the cheek, and my children protested at the unfairness, so I crossed it out.

He writes 17 hours a day, without having to force himself:

> On the contrary, I find it difficult to tell myself that it's already late and I must go to bed. I try to stop at a point of suspense, because I continue dreaming about what happened that day in

the book. In order to be willing to tear three whole years from my life, the text must surprise me daily, and make me laugh and cry. I need the fuel of curiosity, otherwise I cannot write.

His large study is in the basement of his three-storey house in Mevasseret, an affluent suburb of Jerusalem. 'I write out of the Id, from the lower ground floor, and live in the Super-Ego, the top floor', he paraphrases Freud jokingly. But he writes his books mainly outdoors. He takes his notebook and drives to his secret valley, not far from home. He puts the notebook on the ground and walks in circles for five or six hours:

It looks sort of crazy. When a sentence comes into my mind, I sit on the ground and write it by hand. The drafts on the computer only come later, at home, when I develop a scene from ten different viewpoints, until the strongest side emerges. I eat a lot when I write, so I bring sandwiches along.

In winter days, when he can't go out, he's like a lion in his den, walking for hours around his study. To finish *Be My Knife* he rented a small apartment in a new immigrant's neighbourhood in the northern hilly town of Zefat:

I left a black scorch mark on the carpet, in the shape of a circle. I was alone. I didn't go to the balcony not even once in eight days; I followed my internal clock, dropping down for four hours of sleep, and getting up to continue writing, regardless if it was three at night or four in the afternoon. It is the ideal state for writing; I never feel that I turn my back on the world when I write. I only feel sorrow for missing the small joys of my family, but I surrender to a stronger voice that demands my full attention. Writing a book is like hiding a Jewish family during the Holocaust. They just wouldn't survive if I didn't sneak them all their needs: a philosophy of life, ideology, ideas, character, morals, as well as the most mundane things, like what they eat and where they empty their bowels. They need me, like a baby that would die if he were not fed. The most wonderful and frightening feeling is that it's my story. Without me it will not be, no other person in the world can tell it.

*Be My Knife* is a quote from Kafka's letter to his married love, Milena: 'Love means that you are the knife with which I probe inside my soul'. Grossman's book is a novel in letters: Yair, a married man of 33, spots a tall, curly-haired, unknown woman at his school reunion, standing by a man, probably her husband. Yair hears the man's coarse laughter when speaking about a genetic experiment that makes hares lose their foetuses. Yair observes the woman recoiling, hugging herself and smiling a broken smile. Without exchanging a word with her, he senses that he and that woman were both woven from the same yarn, and she is bound to understand him. Throughout his life he has felt vulnerable, exposed, more feminine than masculine. He traces her name and address, secretly rents a post office box, and only two days later sends her his first letter. He dictates his terms: a relationship of words and imagination only, limited by time. 'Sex, not religion, is the opium of the masses', he eventually says, explaining his recoiling from physical contact, which, he believes, distorts the intimacy created in a clean soul-to-soul encounter. To his surprise, she accepts.

– *'You describe marriage as "Two people watching a very sluggish rite, the execution of a much loved person". These are very harsh words from a married man'.*

'Marriage has a tremendous power; to live with one person and touch life through him, pass all ages with him, and experience his transformations. But there's another side too: it's a defined relationship that you lose yourself in. When two loving people are bottled up together in the jar of marriage, every deep breath that the one takes, robs the other, and there is petty bargaining with the person one is supposed to love best. Like accountants, each side keeps the balance, not just who earns more and who works harder, but who's more adventurous in bed. Even the genes that each one contributed to the family bank are somehow counted. Sometimes, the relationship with a spouse is fossilized in a way that paralyses both. You look at it and your heart breaks. You need a knife to sharpen you, and sometimes an outsider is the answer'.

– *'Are you advocating infidelity?'*

'I do not think that Yair is unfaithful. If I knew that my partner is faithful to me just because we signed a contract, it is a fidelity that will not satisfy me. Yair identified in another person something that he needs very much, and his life would not be worth living without. How can he be deprived of it? The real fidelity is to be true to yourself. Very often, people marry for the wrong reasons, and Yair wants to do the right thing at last, and love someone with no boundaries. Aren't we all yearning for it to happen?'

Grossman began to write *Be My Knife* in 1987, wishing to tell a story about the discovery of love and sexuality. After a year he felt that before looking outwards to write about relationships, he first had to travel inwards and know himself. After seven years – and two other books – he was ready. The grown-up Yair of *Be My Knife* could have been the young Aharon, the protagonist of *The Book of Intimate Grammar*. The two of them are very much like the child Grossman was, 'an egg without a shell, a man with a thin skin, and I feel that life scratches me'.

– *'The years didn't toughen you, and grow a shell around you?'*
'I cannot and do not wish to grow a shell. On the contrary, as I grow older, my defense is to detach myself from strangers. Only with my dear ones – my wife, my children and two or three friends – can I be bare'.

– *'I suppose that, unlike Yair, who experienced his father's brown belt intimately, you were not a battered child'.*
'No, but every child is battered in some way. I was a very difficult child to raise. I felt I had to defend my privacy against an invasion of a misunderstanding society. I was showered with love, and at the same time, unloved and misunderstood. I love my parents, and I'm not sure I would have done better raising a child like myself'.

Grossman's wife Michal is a psychologist, and they met during their army service. They have three children. It's a quiet, intimate marriage of people who feel like allies in an unfriendly world. 'Half our life we are intimidated by our parents, and half our life we're intimidated by our children. I want to believe that one marries a spouse he can be open with'.

– '**Be My Knife** *takes place in Jerusalem, but does not touch upon the harsh reality of daily life under the terror of the Intifada'.*
'I wrote about two people falling in love, and they are blind to poli-

tics and national conflicts. Sometimes this kind of love is a way of escaping reality, and saying "I" and not the public "Us". Nevertheless, there's something typical Israeli in Yair: he lives a tense, tough life, due to an anxious, totalitarian education, which deprives one of privacy. Yair asks Miriam to be the knife that will cut a glued envelope, a cataract that has built up around him. He wants her to roll away the stones that block the flow of the spring. It takes a lot of courage to do so. Look how many people are trapped inside a shell, look at our country, trapped inside its anxieties and its history, and when we are offered a chance to breathe a different air, we ignore it'.

– *'The house is burning and you write love letters?'*
'My first son was born in 1982, the year of the Lebanon War, and I spent many days writing essays and letters, participated in demonstrations, and travelled frequently to the West Bank, to nourish a dialogue with the Palestinians. I needed to feel that I did all I could, so that when my son turns 18 and is drafted to the army, the political climate will improve. I behaved like a fireman, rushing from one crisis to the other, but one can't surrender all his life to sounding the siren, wearing a helmet and operating the hose. People should write love letters and live and learn. We shouldn't forget that normal life is what we're trying to protect. Our tragedy is that too much energy is invested in the outer shell, and I'm afraid that eventually we'll become an armour with no knight inside'.

Already, at four years old, it dawned on him acutely and concretely that all humans must die.

It scared me terribly, and since then I've been living with a constant awareness of death. I live as if I'll die tomorrow, and each day must be the most exciting and significant and fun. I do not postpone things, and do not waste time. Most people are stingy with their money; I'm stingy with my time, which makes me sort of unbearable in the eyes of many people. We're emerging out of a darkness of a million years, then there's a short flash of light and then we sink again into eternal darkness. I do not console myself with the thought of reincarnation, there's no second term to life. What we have in this world is the beginning and the end. What one doesn't do now, he never will. Finality is a very rich fuel, and if there's something that can sum up what

I'm doing, it is the urge to save the routine from its dreariness, to put a diamond in the tediousness of life by a good story.


## TRANSLATIONS INTO ENGLISH

Grossman, D., *The Yellow Wind* [*Hazman Hatzahov*; trans. H. Watzman] (London: Jonathan Cape, 1988/New York: Farrar Straus Giroux, 1998/New York: Picador, 1999).
—— *See Under: Love* [*Ayen Erech: Ahava*; trans. B. Rosenberg] (New York: Farrar Straus Giroux, 1989/New York: Picador, 2001/London: Vintage, 1999).
—— *The Smile of the Lamb* [*Hiyuch Hagdi*; trans. B. Rosenberg] (New York: Farrar Straus Giroux, 1990/London: Jonathan Cape, 1991).
—— *Sleeping on a Wire: Conversations with Palestinians in Israel* [*Nochahim-Nifkadim*; trans. H. Watzman] (New York: Farrar Straus Giroux, 1992/London: Jonathan Cape, 1993).
—— *The Book of Intimate Grammar* [*Sefer ha-dikduk ha-penimi*; trans. B. Rosenberg] (New York: Farrar Straus Giroux, 1994).
—— *The Zigzag Kid* [trans. B. Rosenberg] (New York: Farrar Straus Giroux, 1997/London: Bloomsbury, 1997).
—— *Duel* [*Du-Krav*; trans. B. Rosenberg] (London: Bloomsbury, 1999).
—— *Be My Knife* [*Shetihi Li Ha-sakin*; trans. M. Gurantz] (New York: Farrar Straus Giroux, 2001/London: Bloomsbury, 2002).
—— *Death as a Way of Life* [articles; trans. H. Watzman] (London: Bloomsbury, 2003).
—— *Someone to Run With* [*Mishe'hu Larutz Ito*; trans. V. Almog and M. Gurantz] (New York: Farrar, Straus & Giroux, 2003/London: Bloomsbury, 2003).

# CHAPTER SEVENTEEN

# Ronit Matalon
## (1959– )

# Reminiscences of a Street Cat

Everything, even the most personal, becomes political for Ronit Matalon. Speaking of her father's death on 29 September 2000, she immediately comments that it happened on the very day that Ariel Sharon provokingly toured Temple Mount:

> A few hours after I buried my father, the Intifada riots began. It was the eve of the Jewish New Year, and the festival annulled the Shiv'a, the customary seven days of mourning. I was relieved, as I felt I had been grieving my father since the day I was born. Some people affect by their presence, my father affected us by his absence.

Felix Matalon was a lone wolf, an eternal nomad, and a journalist who organized the first workers' demonstrations in the newly born State of Israel. He dwelled in the slums of Tel Aviv out of socialist principles, published pamphlets advocating rights for Sephardi Jews, and strove for the foundation of a left-wing Sephardi party. 'Since he was an atheist, he was blind to the Sephardi fundamental affinity with tradition, and their alienation towards the newer religions like Socialism and Liberalism'.

In his last years, Felix Matalon became weaker and weaker. Lack of movement was like death to him, and he gradually lost his will to live. At the nursing home, he used to tune his radio to sermons from

the Koran, 'because his roots were more Muslim than Jewish. What
a pity that it was not my father, the Pro-Arabic, who visited Temple
Mount, and that Sharon did not stay instead on his ranch'.

Matalon asked not to be interviewed at home, where she lives with
her husband, the psychoanalyst Professor Emanuel Berman, and
with her son and daughter. The well-known photograph of Virginia
Wolf is hovering in the room of her own, a few minutes' walk away.
Alongside are photos of her children and of writers that she
admires. 'Aside from the biological family, there is the intellectual
family that one assembles for himself'. Until seven years ago, she
worked at home:

> But you know how it is: you sit to write, and jump to switch the
> washing machine off, to put a casserole on the stove. Nowadays,
> I like the idea of leaving home at eight o'clock every morning
> and going to my studio.

And she cuddles up in her blue revolving office chair. She is dark
and petite, her bare feet folded beneath her, their nails lacquered in
silver, her black eyes glowing mischievously.

I meant to begin with 'She was born in 1959'; but it almost did not
happen. Her mother was already struggling with two children, a
mountain of debts and an absent husband, when she found herself
pregnant again: 'I am the accident, I am the abortion that never
took place', says Matalon.

– *'How did you find out?'*
'They both told me that, when I was very young. They always told
me everything. It did not frighten me, it was like a fairy tale about
me, which had a magical element: the two women on a dark night,
in a hut, and Grandma recounting a dream, pleading with mother
to continue with the pregnancy. "Have that child for my sake",
Grandma said, "it will bring us luck". I'm the result of the dilemma
between the rational deed and the moral one'.

Matalon plugged her own birth into her first novel, *The One Facing
Us*:

> Mother had gone through seven abortions, she would get rid of

them as if they were kittens: like kittens she would get rid of them, get up and go to work. Father would go away from time to time, disappearing in European capitals and later on in Africa, sending newspaper clippings and small shell boxes, ivories, full with memoirs. She wanted to get rid of this one as well. Nona would not let her: 'Don't get rid of it, give it to me to bring luck', she pleaded for a whole night, rubbing mother's long bathrobe's belt. She gave it to her. Went to work in rich people's homes, caring for their dogs while they were abroad. She nearly strangled one of them once.

– *'Were you angry with your mother?'*
'I understood her. It broke my heart to think of the unbearable situation she found herself in. This sort of story told to you about yourself, does a lot of things to your soul. It makes you feel that your existence was not obvious, but it also creates a sense that you were very much wanted'.

Her parents were born into distinguished, affluent Egyptian-Jewish families. Upon immigrating to Israel in 1949, her mother had to wash her own lingerie for the first time in her life; her hands bled because they were so delicate, and the laundry soap bar coarse and rigid. But, having no profession, the only living she could make was by cleaning other peoples' homes:

> When I was young, I was ashamed of her work, but, later, was ashamed of being ashamed, and angry at the social climate that made me ashamed. Mother always said that work is never a disgrace; it is a disgrace to beg. I have never met anyone who laboured as hard as she did, working in several places a day; each job meant to support one of her children.

On the chest drawers is a framed photograph of a beautiful and strong woman, Grandma Esther, almost blind due to a degenerative eye disease. She lived in a near-by hut and raised Ronit. The grandmother was educated in a convent in Alexandria, played the piano and wished that Ronit would attend a prestigious French convent school in Jaffa:

> Financially, it was an unrealistic dream, and I went to the local Hebrew school. Whenever I came to her after school, she would

say in Arabic, 'You have lightened up our room'. She gave me the feeling that a family is where you are loved for your sheer existence, not depending on your achievements.

Grandma Esther died in 1985. Ten years later, the 17-year-old, opinionated and alert protagonist of *The One Facing Us*, would be named after her.

Ronit Matalon grew up in Ganei Tikva, 'Gardens of Hope', which had 'no gardens and no hope', a run-down enclave surrounded by affluent suburbs. Streets without lights or sidewalks, a scorching ground devoid of shade. In the wooden shacks, children slept crowded on one bed, stuck together like animal cubs.

Most of the families came from North Africa, most mothers cleaned the homes of rich European-born Israelis. Most fathers did not work, most older brothers slept until two in the afternoon, and in school they would beat their teachers. Says Matalon:

[It was] a suburb that was always on the verge of criminality. From a very young age I knew a lot about the infinite ways of wretchedness, evilness and cruelty. I was always busy with survival, going through tests of loyalties and blackmails, fighting for social acceptance and pretending to be a tough cookie, beating and being beaten. I still loved the street life, as I was free of supervision. The street-girl within me did not disappear; she simply went through several transformations. I cannot have my freedom of movement constrained, and I constantly wish to keep on moving. I am not afraid of violence, and I always refuse to see myself as a victim. I love getting lost in the streets, engaging in conversations with complete strangers. But as much as I can become unbalanced and moody, carried away by excessive excitements, when it comes to my children or to my writing, I am sober and precise.

In their flimsy two-bedroom shack, their toilet shared with their neighbours, the walls were so thin that once, as Ronit's older brother explained to her an exercise in mathematics, and he got upset by her ignorance and hit the plywood walls, his fist went through the other side:

The roof was leaking, and for an entire winter we would prepare coffee holding an umbrella, because mother wanted to renovate the kitchen, but there was no money left for fixing the roof. Nevertheless, it was a wonderful home.

Only when she was five or six years old did she see her father for the first time, when he came home for a few days.

> I always identified with orphans, although I wasn't one. We never knew when he would return, and I was in a constant state of expectation. When at last he opened the door, it was like an opera singer, who turns up to perform his aria and then disappears.

She used to sit on a hill overlooking the bus station, and wait days in vain for him. To pass the time, she would play her favourite game: collecting colourful flower petals, burying them in the sand and putting fragments of glass bottles over them, like tombstones. Through the glass, the flowers would be reflected, enlarged and distorted. Then she would dig her own flower grave, feigning surprise with the newfound treasure. 'The act of hiding something from yourself, changing its form and then searching for it, is very much related to what I do in literature'. Her parents divorced when she was eight:

> My father continued wandering like some sort of a Ulysses, a nomad who brought with him the scents of the big world. He was a true non-conformist that could not be caged. Often, the absentee is more powerful than the one that is present, and my father created a lot of energies and passions by his absences as well as by his presence.

At times she admired her father, at times was afraid to resemble him:

> I never reconciled with him, and I never detached myself from him. His image has been within me ever since I began to write, and it changed phases. In my early short stories, my father is portrayed as a pathetic and ridiculous political activist, the failure of a man who built towers in thin air, and destroyed his family for nothing. Today I respect his choices, even though I find it hard to understand where his paternal instinct was.

Happily for me, I had a chance to show him the things I had written about him. He responded with reserved happiness. He had always known that I was a chip off the old block.

It is not accidental that later in life, she did not take the name of either one of her two husbands, but instead held on to her father's name, Matalon, which means 'a sailor' in Ladino:

I did not have many things to take from him, no memories, no material assets, so at least I wanted his name. Only recently I was pleasantly surprised to learn that in the Muslim world, a daughter traditionally takes the name of her father, and only the very rebellious take their husband's.

At 14, she was assigned to an occupational school, to be trained as a laboratory assistant:

This is how the establishment treated Sephardi children, and it never changed, turning us into seamstresses and hairdressers, mechanics and electricians, blocking our way to university, and to high-status professions. It was unthinkable to rebel against the system, but I did, and luckily, my mother supported me, and somehow managed to pull strings and find me another school.

Ronit is the only member of her family who made it to university. Her sister, Alexandra, is a shopwindow dresser, and her brother, Yaakov, a constructer of billboards:

As the youngest daughter of an immigrants' family, and the only one born in Israel, the expectations of the entire family were set on me. Obviously, I have guilt feelings for my siblings, because life smiled on me more than it did on them. I feel the burden, the guilt of the survivor; because one wishes to be like the people he loves.

While a student at Tel Aviv University, reading philosophy and literature, she published her first story, but waited for years until she felt ripe enough to publish a short story collection, *Strangers At Home*. The Matalons were amazing storytellers, with a taste for the fantastic, each having his own version of the family drama:

This is the first form of literature I encountered, a Rashomon of viewpoints that I'm still trying to decipher. Since I began to write, I have been preoccupied with my family and with the effort to understand the world through it. My literary tastes are similar, I love the great family novel: *Anna Karenina*, *War and Peace*; mostly Russian literature. I'm a person of contrasts, a prim little lady and a street cat, because reality spoke to me in many different voices.

Her first novel, *The One Facing Us*, was published when she was 35 years old:

It was certainly not a meteoric breakthrough, and I am thankful for it. Success is heavier than the load of failure. An early-age success, when your personality is not yet defined, may shatter you and make you bitter later on.

– *'Did you triumph over your biography?'*

'Not entirely. There are pits in one's soul that cannot be bridged over. Events from early childhood, fractures that you are trying to mend throughout your life, and they are not entirely curable. In order to survive a past as complicated as mine, you have to change constantly; otherwise you are lost, doomed. A miserable childhood is rarely the ignition, or the fuel, of a writer, or else the majority of humanity would be artists. Writing demands an enormous ability to be alone, to have a deep yearning for that thin border between the permitted and the forbidden, between the lies and the truth. My biography provided me with a sort of flexibility, to move between different situations, feeling comfortable in several environments, doing a lot of things all at once'.

Matalon has reservations about the term 'the congregational rupture':

A rupture assumes that something was once whole, but there was never a homogenous collective in Israel. Nowadays, the Sephardi Israelis are more widely represented politically, but there aren't many academics, and by all parameters of success, such as ownership of apartments, education, income – the gaps are still outrageous.

She follows in her father's political footsteps, and strongly criticizes the Sephardi religious political party, Shas:

> They turn insults into an ideology, and try to capitalize on the fact that North African Jews were sprayed with DDT against lice when they arrived in Israel in its early years. I think that they deserve their equal share in the economic and social cake, not because they had been ill-treated, but because they are a part of society. When one speaks from the victim's stance, one internalises the aggressor's verdict.

In 1988–89, the first years of the Intifada, Matalon left her young son at home, driving every week in her unprotected car to the Gaza Strip and the West Bank. Speaking fluent Arabic from childhood, she interviewed Palestinians for the *Ha'Aretz* daily. She met families whose sons had been killed by the Israeli Army, whose daughter was blinded by a rubber bullet. Many times, she stayed the night at the house of one of her Palestinian contacts – who later became her friend – and they were her houseguests in Tel Aviv. In one of her articles she wrote:

> After a while it seemed that this entire room, full of thick cigarette smoke, is the photograph of the dead boy. His sister Samia hurries up and brings more photographs, frightful, macabre: for an entire night her brother bled heavily on the kitchen floor until he died. Death, so it seems, is folded in every uttering, in each of their gestures, in each reference to the past or the future. Death is a criterion for everything, and paradoxically, it is the most vital, vivid part of life.

'I identified with the Palestinian cause, not least because of my Oriental background', she says:

> The Arab world never frightened me, my parents grew up in Egypt, and the language was natural for me. My grandma used to say, 'You must never forget anybody, especially the ones who are easy to forget'. I learned at home never to ignore the weak, and always knew that one can easily become the weak. I cannot identify with my nation's just cause to be planted in our historic homeland, and not identify with the uprooted, the deported Palestinian fugitives. But seeing the 'Other' and his fears does

not ease my own hysterical fears as an Israeli, that seven Arab states wish to demolish us. I sympathize with Ulysses' desire to return home and believe that Israel should morally acknowledge the wish of the Palestinian refugees to return to their pre-1948 homes in Israel. It doesn't mean that we'll evacuate our homes and let them have it. Like the Arabs I will cling to my little haven in central Tel Aviv, and bulldozers would have to drag me away from here.

When her Palestinian contact was murdered by Arab militants for co-operating with Israel, she stopped going to Gaza, trying to keep in touch by phone, but the conversations died out, as both sides felt that words were limited and hopeless, and could not break the walls of the deep pit each side was buried in:

> I'm afraid that the Israeli–Palestinian confrontation will continue for another hundred years; we will 'shave off' a row of houses in a refugee camp, because they are firing at our settlements, and they will blow up another bus, and we'll retaliate, and they will take revenge. Perhaps in 2100, when we are all exhausted by dreadful decades of massacres, and forget how it all began, there will be peace.

In 2000, her family spent a six-month sabbatical in New York:

> I always had a fantasy that I am a citizen of the world, and perhaps I could follow my maternal instinct, to guard my children, and move them away from the dangers of Israel. But in the USA, I discovered how much of a native Israeli I really am, short-tempered, emotional. New York is very attractive, but I need the commotion of Israel like oxygen.


## TRANSLATIONS INTO ENGLISH

Matalon, R. *The One Facing Us* [*Ze Im Hapanim Eleinu*; trans. M. Weinstein] (New York: Henry Holt and Co., 1998).

# CHAPTER EIGHTEEN

# Zeruyah Shalev
## (1959– )

# A Collector of Catastrophes

Her elongated face radiates tortured beauty. She seems like a scared bird fluttering in the palm of the hand, shivering at her own shadow, and – as she described in one of her novels – of the kind that makes you want to protect her, to make her cover herself lest she catches a cold, hide herself from the sun lest she burns.

Huge oils made by her mother, painter Rika Shalev, decorate her living room. In one of them, the pregnant Zeruyah in a flowery dress is sprawled on a sofa. There were years that she made her living as a painters' model. The artists were intrigued by her Modgliani face and by her waist-long raven hair. She comes across as a mixture of intellect and eroticism; hiding, when bewildered, behind her mane as a veil. So is her writing simultaneously introverted and provocative. 'My novels are not the mirror of my life, but of my nightmares', she says. 'My life, though not very good and happy, is much brighter than the reality of my novels'.

Zeruyah Shalev was born in 1959 in Kibbutz Kinneret on the banks of the Sea of Galilee, and she is a first cousin of novelist Meir Shalev. With her older brother, Aner, now a novelist and a professor of mathematics, Zeruyah grew up on the premises of Beit Berl Teachers' College in the Sharon, where their father taught:

It was a lonely childhood in an isolated out-of-town place, there were no other children around but us, but it had its own magic, being completely cut off from urbanity. I would wander about, daydream and invent stories. On winter nights I would go out to gaze at the roving clouds, watching them, enchanted, as others watch a movie. My only playmates were cats, we had about ten of them who ruled the yard and jumped on us the moment we opened the door.

While other children went to sleep with 'Snow White and the Seven Dwarfs' or 'Hansel and Gretel', Zeruyah's bedtime storybook was not the Brothers Grimm but the Bible:

We inhaled neither the sweet idealization of fairy tales, nor their frightening monstrosity. I loved to hear the one about Joseph and his brothers, for its happy ending; or about Hanna, the mother of Samuel the Prophet, who was barren for many years like my own mother. The Bible gave our childhood a sense of reality and authenticity; our dreams were inhabited not by wicked witches or wolves in disguise, but by realistic problems like sibling rivalry, power struggles or childlessness.

Her most pleasant childhood memories are from age four, when her father read to her and her five-year-old brother from *Agnon*; texts not meant for such young children. For an encore, they would call out as a chorus, 'Ag-non! Ag-non!' – just as other children root for a football team. When she was eight, her father moved on to Franz Kafka, and she remembers *The Trial*, *Metamorphoses* and *Behind the Locked Gate*.

She has been writing poetry ever since she learned to put words together. Some years back, she found her first notebook: tragic poems about cats and kittens who were run over by cars or succumbed to winter or illness. She feels gloomy and is always ready for the worst – her novels reflect her pull towards the dark side of life:

But it's not my biography that made me pessimistic. With the same lonely childhood surrounded by cats, a totally different lady could have emerged. It seems that my melancholy is in my genes.

Her father, Mordechai Shalev, is a critic and an essayist, an ascetic man of rigid principles and integrity and astute self-criticism. Zeruyah Shalev is still in awe and refuses to speak about him, adhering to the restraint he imposed on himself.

In her first novel, *I Danced, I Stood*, the heroine puts her father on trial for caressing her on her head:

> A double charge: for caressing me on my hair just once in my life, and for daring to caress me at all.
> 'Did he leave his hand for longer than was customary?', the lawyer asked.
> 'No, he took away his hand as if he were scorched by fire'.
> 'So, why are you suing him?', he again refused to understand.
> 'Don't you think it's a crime, to take away your hand so quickly from a 12-and-a-half-year-old girl?'

Shalev settles the account with parents in general, and not just with her own:

> Parenthood is a no-win situation. We do not become better mothers than our mothers were to us. We are not taught to be parents; the only role we learn is to be a child in our own nuclear family. When you become a mom, the child in you must wait in the corner until you bring up the child you gave birth to. Most women do not admit it; we all pretend motherhood is a ball. It's sublime to give life, but in return, you must bury yourself. From the moment my daughter was born, I felt that my whole life was going to be determined by her dictum, and that I would have to behave to such perfection, that it would make me neglect myself. Nothing comes easy to me; everything involves a lot of effort and internal conflict. My girlfriends may cook a dinner party in 30 minutes; I have to prepare a month in advance, consulting with 50 friends over the phone.

She speaks timidly trying to protect her loved ones, her words much softer than the sharp accusations that her novels present. She wrote in her first novel:

> If your parents screwed you up, you are screwed up. If they did you in, you are done for. If they cooked you, you are cooked. If they shrunk you, you're shrunk. If they blew you up, you are blown up.

In her teens she planned to become a psychologist, but while dealing with soldiers' welfare during her army service she felt herself collapsing under the strain, and realized that she was not fit for it. She finished her BA and MA in Bible Studies with distinction, and became an editor in the prestigious publishing house Keter. She first published a poem when she was 17 in the literary supplement of *Ha'Aretz* newspaper, but postponed her first book of poems for another 11 years. The book, *An Easy Target for Snipers*, won her excellent reviews and three literary prizes.

She first married at 22, and divorced after a year. Her second marriage produced a daughter, but Zeruyah was restless. Long before her marriage fell apart, she chanced upon a woman, who had decided to follow her heart. Since this woman thought that life would not be worth living without the lover, she struggled for a divorce; but, in return, her husband made her sign away her right to her children, her home and property. Not long after, the lover beat her up and deserted her, and she was left devoid of everything: no children, no husband, and no love. This woman's fate seeped into Zeruyah Shalev's consciousness:

> I'm a collector of catastrophes. Every shocking tale of other people's reality becomes my own. I went on with my married life, working and raising up my daughter, but in my heart, I began lamenting what I might leave behind, if I too decided to leave my husband. I remember waking up with an appalling phrase ringing in my head: 'When you leave your child, you're endlessly pregnant, you're walking with it inside you all the time'. I understood that only when you're about to lose your child, do you feel his or her existence.

A fortunate mishap launched her triumphant prose-writing career. She was due to meet an author whose text she was editing, and for two hours she waited in the café. When he failed to arrive, she took a paper napkin, and began to scribble, and in no time, she had ten scrawled pages.

> It was a marvellous feeling, because I had never written prose before, never thought I could. It erupted from my guts – the way I write poetry – by impulse, never knowing if I will ever write another line. It was a fascinating voyage. Every time I stopped, I was sure it would not continue. But after a few days, another phrase came. Some passages were practically written in tears.

*– 'And what happened in real life meanwhile?'*
'My marriage fell apart, and I began to explore more deeply my
concept of a family. I was always ambivalent about it. I wanted a
family, but it was a painful infringement upon my privacy. You
marry at 20, at a moment when you feel very close to your spouse,
and some years later you have no idea what you're doing with this
stranger. It's a race where two people hit the road, but do not reach
the finishing line together'.

That was the catalyst for *I Danced, I Stood*, a violent novel, with
black humour and blunt sexuality:

> The conclusion is very pessimistic, because the heroine leaves all
> the people that were a part of her adult life, returns to her child-
> hood home and regresses to her parents' lap to become a baby
> again. Judging by the few couples I know that do have a success-
> ful marriage, the secret is to lower your expectations, to set a list
> of priorities, to insist only on the essential, and let go of the
> superfluous. That's what people blessed with common sense do,
> and that's what my heroine could not do.

In the final stages of her marriage, Shalev wrote an enthusiastic
review of a poetry book by novelist Ayal Megged. Having read the
compliments, Megged, who like Shalev belongs to a family of
writers, called her. Falling in love, they divorced their spouses and
got married, bringing up three children by their previous marriages,
and their son. 'In a class meeting in the presence of all the parents,
each child was asked to describe the favorite pastime of the family',
Shalev recalls:

> When it was my daughter's turn, she said, 'The hobby of our
> family is divorce'. I was speechless with shame, and mustered
> the courage to try and correct the record publicly, 'Well, we
> probably also like to get married'.

Matrimony is the main theme in Shalev's writing, and in retro-
spect she thinks that for most of her life, she's been seeking protection rather than love:

> Some men like to protect women, but they demand a very dear
> price: you are cast in the role of the weak one. In most of these

relationships I could eventually get what I wanted, but I didn't like the image of myself that stared at me from the mirror. I've never been on my own, I just moved on from one marriage to the other. It takes much more courage to be alone, than to marry and divorce two or three times.

Living with a novelist, and writing about marriage, brought Shalev and Megged's marriage under scrutiny:

It's a clash of two conflicting dreams: on the one hand, you dream to be with a person who is made from the same stuff as you are and understands what you are going through, but on the other hand, you wish to have a practical spouse who takes care of you while you are immersed in your writing. Every writer secretly wishes he had a person less egocentric than him. In that respect, we were both disappointed.

In 1997, Shalev stormed the bestseller charts in Israel, and later in Germany, with *Love Life*. Yaara, the heroine, is a graduate student, married to a nice, goodhearted, but unexciting, man. When she meets Aryeh, a mysterious and arrogant older man, and a friend of her parents, she cannot help but follow him into a relationship of lust and humiliation that undermines not only her marriage but also her shaky academic career. The destructive, often erotically repulsive affair also liberates Yaara, and makes her define her identity and fathom her parents' past. For the first time in her life she learns of the fatal bond between her mother and Aryeh and understands her brother's death and the basis of her parents' dysfunctional marriage.

Shalev used her academic expertise in Jewish theology, to draw allegories between the heroine's crumbling marriage, and the destruction of the Holy Temple in Jerusalem 2000 years ago. The semi-incestuous affair that the promiscuous Yaara has with her mother's lover is not only Shalev's homage to Agnon's *In the Prime of her Life*, but also a manifestation of the biblical metaphor of the Nation of Israel as a beautiful and ungrateful young woman who fornicates under her God and Master. Like so many of the biblical heroes and heroines, Yaara has a mission to fulfil – to repair the past, and correct the future.

Shalev repeated her success in 2001, with *Husband and Wife*. This is the story of a symbiotic relationship: Naama wakes up one morning and discovers that Udi, her husband, a tour guide who made the Bible his travel book, has been paralyzed by a mysterious illness and cannot get out of bed. She tries to cure him as if curing her own body, and is shattered when her husband deserts her and their daughter for the young woman who tried to heal him using Tibetan methods: Shalev's biblical imagery in this modern story, reflects a deeper dimension, leaving the Law of the Lord, and following the ways of the Gentiles. ' I burst into tears describing their break-up, but I felt that breaking up is inevitable, and I hoped that the sorrow she was experiencing, and I experience through her, will be transformed into strength', Shalev says.

She identified with her two heroines, who represent different ways of thinking: Yaara of *Love Life* wants to shatter her marriage and break free of it, while Naama of *Husband and Wife* tries to save it at all costs, but it crumbles in her hands. Shalev says she's attracted to extreme situations since they are more powerful; realistic, mediocre situations bore her.

For many years, she says, she was dependant on men's opinion of her. Only if she was loved, did she feel worthy. Today, her whole perception of marriage has changed. She wonders whether it would be better to have less of love, and more of friendship, since there is so much destruction and anxiety and frustration in love, while friendship is all about acceptance and support:

> The desire to be together continually, and take on the problems of the other, and that he will take on your problems, is an illusion that is shattered quickly. It's probably better to walk around the house with a small wall around you, to remember that your spouse is not you; he's a separate entity. When you live together, even a bad mood of the other penetrates you, and then you feel deserted or guilty or threatened. My heroine understands that she must let go of the obsessive wish to change her husband. You must let go, in order to win. You cannot change him, you can only change yourself, and you must deal with yourself and not with him.

The insight and common sense gained by time, with which she imbued her heroines, is that it's much healthier to be separate, each taking care of his or her life and expectations:

> If once I viewed a good relationship as one in which two people do everything together and support each other, today I hope for two separate tree-trunks, growing side by side.

## TRANSLATIONS INTO ENGLISH

Shalev, Z., *Love Life* [*Hayei Ahava*; trans. D. Bilu] (New York: Grove/Atlantic, Inc., 2000).

—— *Husband and Wife* [*Baal Veisha*; trans. D. Bilu] (New York: Grove/Atlantic, Inc., 2002).

# CHAPTER NINETEEN

# Orly Castel-Bloom
## (1960– )

# Between Motherhood and Madness

I went to an old carpenter and I asked him to glue the child to my back. First of all, I would not see him; the layer of glue would separate us, so that I would not really touch him. Secondly, he would grow on my back, slowly turning into a part of me and I into a part of him. And then, when the boundaries between him and me were completely broken open, I could swallow his existence and forget him, and I would not have to worry so much again. And – as for the not particularly aesthetic hunch – I did not give a damn. I knew whoever wants me would take me as I am, and that if my hunch disturbed him – then he should go and fuck some other woman.

That was the original solution for the crushing burden of maternal obligation that the heroine of Orly Castel-Bloom's novel *Dolly City* found – and that, after already having installed grids on the windows of her thirty-seventh-floor apartment, as well as on the apertures of the sinks and bathtub, so that the child would not slip into the sewage. She invented a thousand other tricks to dodge the death sentence that hovers above a child's head from the moment of birth.

Orly Castel-Bloom was first introduced to maternal anxiety when she gave birth to her daughter:

After just three days at the hospital they send you home, and I was in panic. How on earth was I supposed to know what to do? I suffered from over-anxiety. For every cough I would give her a thorough check-up, imagining all sorts of illnesses and deformities. Psychologists say that this manifests some kind of repressed aggressiveness, a fear of my own violence. Some mothers beat their child with murderous blows, and others abuse with over-protectiveness. Can someone tell us what is normal concern? If everything is about quantities, let the experts publish a chart, and say that a 100 cc. is the right amount of concern; above this – the mother should go to therapy, higher than that, the child must be given for adoption, and below it, just sent away to a foster family.

She named the heroine of her novel 'Dolly' rather than 'Orly', but the similarity in sound is just one of the clues that Castel-Bloom did not spread too thick a veil to separate fact from fiction:

I play with my biography when I write. I enjoy showing my real self for a glimpse of a moment, and then change some details and turn into a different person altogether. Like Dolly, I suffer from 'The Infinite Possibilities Disease', when the brain constantly invents scenarios. I experience many parallel realities simultaneously; I can enjoy the sight of a boat floating calmly by, and at the same time, see it sinking. It's enough that I think of the possibility that the house may be burning, for me to jump and dial the Fire Brigade.

Orly began her writing career in late 1985, during her pregnancy, but after only three books, when her daughter was eight, she wrote *Dolly City*:

All those years I tormented myself; you are a mother, how come you don't write about motherhood. In *Where am I?*, the heroine is twice divorced, with no children; one could think you are single. You are distant from yourself, if you cannot touch something that is so important to you. When I finally was ready, I said to myself, 'Missy, this time you will let all the crap come out, the dark anxieties, the perversions, that damned responsibility that could drive you insane'. I sat down to write Dolly with a pen and paper, because half of my previous book got deleted from my computer, and I could not risk losing this book as well. Before popping out to the supermarket, I would check over and over again that I indeed turned off the gas, as I was afraid that the house would be set on fire, and the manuscript burned down. I wrote it with red ink, but it was blood. I felt that this time I am inside the guts, that I am slaughtering holy cows. I was shivering while writing, and I'm glad I purged it out, because these are dangerous, poisonous materials.

When we met, the memory of the Israeli mother who, a week before, drowned her two little girls in the bathtub, was hovering in the air. The newspapers carried more horrific stories: an Indian mother decapitated her children with a knife; a French couple tied up their three-year-old son's penis so he would not wet his pants, and the boy died; a 50-year-old American maliciously infected hundreds of young boys with HIV; and, in Brazil, children were kidnapped and killed, their organs being sold for transplants. It seemed that Castel-Bloom finds the horrors she plants in her books, not in her blazing imagination, but rather in reality:

> The phrase, 'How could she do that, she is a mother?', makes me laugh, as if Holy Motherhood is a guarantee for safety. I explore the boundaries of human evil, and how far can maternal evilness go. *Dolly City* is about deterioration into madness. Due to her over-protectiveness, Dolly abuses her child.

Orly Castel-Bloom was born in Tel Aviv in 1960, to parents who emigrated from Egypt in 1949. Until she was four, she only knew French, which was her parents' tongue, and her acrobatic command of Hebrew is derived from her early drive to excel in it, as one masters a foreign language. She attributes almost magical power to words, and her writing resembles a video clip: images chase each other in a rapid, squally, tempo. Fantasy breaks loose, like in cartoons, when a belly splits open and closes like a zip, a roller drives over a person and flattens him out, but soon after, he blows up again and comes back to life.

Critics interpret her hyperactive style as a manifestation of an alienated society, her world is chaotic, fragmented, her writing ironic, so Castel-Bloom surprises me when she confesses that her favourite reading material is history books:

I like reading about the ancient world, about the Israelites during the Greek and Roman Empire. History provides a certainty, stories with a beginning, middle and an ending. It gives me a sense of assurance that the present does not provide me.

Like Dolly's father, Orly's worked for the national airline. Salvo Castel was the paymaster of El Al, and died young of lung cancer:

I tried to make sense of his life and death. His life went wrong, and by planting him into my book, I wanted to pay a tribute to him and leave some record of his existence. He never saw my writing, as I began only after he died. If he were alive, I would not have put a single word on paper. He had some Victorian prudishness about him and I would not dare say the word 'arse' in his presence, and in my writing I use many words blunter than that.

As to her mother, she doesn't read Hebrew well, and hasn't read any of her daughter's books:

She is rather reserved about my occupation. She has been a bankteller for 44 years, and says that books are only dreams, that I should stop dreaming and start working. She thinks I am spoiled, and that my dark moods sprout out of boredom, because I think too much. She urges me to find a proper job, be busy all day long, so I won't have time to think. I'm a bit hurt that she does not acknowledge me, but perhaps it also liberates me.

After her military service, Orly studied filmmaking but dropped out, applied to work as a copywriter, and was rejected. Her life looks as if it was derived from one of her novels:

All of a sudden I was told I was pregnant, and my father was dying of cancer, and I raced against the clock, as I wanted him to see his screwed-up daughter in a white dress and giving birth to his first grandchild.

She married hastily at the rabbinical court and for the customary breaking of a glass – to commemorate the destruction of the

Holy Temple – Orly grabbed the first drinking glass she laid her hand on in her mother's kitchen. It turned out to be too thick, and when the groom, journalist Gadi Bloom, stepped on the glass, he embarrassingly failed to crash it and was injured. He had to be rushed to the emergency clinic to have his foot stitched, and missed the wedding party. 'People consoled us that it indicates a relationship that cannot be broken asunder, but it turned out to be rather the symbol of an ailing marriage'. Characteristically making fiction out of her life, she used the wedding mishap in one of her stories. 'I watch life, and immediately report it in writing. I've been in all sorts of traps, and the lessons that I learn are immediately conveyed to others in the best way I can'.

At 25, she still had no idea what to do with her life:

> I just wanted to stay at home and raise my baby. I didn't want to get up early in the morning, and obey bosses; I just wanted to be left alone. Being a writer seemed to be the perfect solution, the closest thing to doing nothing. It seems to me rather dreamy: what could one want more than to write a not very thick book once in a while, a book that summarizes your emotions, opinions and internal world. Writing is an attempt to find a cure for the malignancy of life, but it has a price, you need courage to plunge into the abyss and rise all the way back. No one can blame me of being a coward.

Two years after her wedding and her father's death, she experienced an existential anxiety. 'There were problems that could be solved quickly, but it took me years. Writing *Dolly City* cured me of maternal anxieties, and for the first time in three years, I burst out laughing'. The release enabled her to get pregnant again and give birth to a son. A short time later, she wrote a story about a couple planning to commit suicide together. The woman died and the man was left handicapped. The neighbours looked at him as if he was guilty of not dying with her, and expected him to complete the act of suicide. But as time passed, he realized that he got by very well without his wife:

> She did not bother him anymore, and slowly, without admitting it to himself out loud, he understood that she was the reason that he wanted to die in the first place, and now that she was dead, and he had done all that he could to die – he felt much

better. No one disturbed him or criticised him. His life were his, no one watched him every day and reproached him about his appearance, or the empty life he was living.

('The Party', in *Free Radicals*)

This was probably a case in which the subconscious writes itself. I did not realize at the time that I was writing about my crumbling marriage. I wrote the story and put it aside. My marriage was deteriorating, but it took me seven more years to admit that I am at my best when I'm on my own, and that institutions are not for me. I had a duty to immunize my children and convey to them that life is not a picnic, but also to protect them from the ugly side of my marriage. The divorce enabled me to be myself, and be a better mother to them.

When she heard the words 'you are hereby permitted for any man', Orly Castel-Bloom felt ecstatically happy:

> I looked at the religious judges at the rabbinical court in Tel Aviv, three bearded, 70-year-old men, muttering, 'permitted, permitted, permitted'. In Hebrew, it is the same word as 'untangling a knot', and I was euphoric, not because I was free for other men, but free from chains and from the need to suffer.

– *'Like Virginia Wolf, what you needed was a room of your own?'*
'At first I thought that I needed a room of my own, then, a flat of my own, and finally I understood that I actually needed a life of my own. Today I feel like a free radical that broke loose, one of those six billion people who wander around the globe. I am an outsider, but this is my way of fitting in. Outside the conjugal cell, I feel much more connected to the rest of humanity, less estranged than before'.

The first thing she did after her divorce, was to read her daughter's encyclopaedia:

> ... to quickly fill my head with all sorts of facts, to reconnect with the reality I had become detached from during my marriage. I had to remind myself of things I had forgotten, because I was occupied with the maintenance of my marriage, which exhausted so much energy.

In that encyclopaedia she discovered a new entry: Castel-Bloom, Orly.

Since her divorce, she has had to support herself and her children. 'I cannot rely on the food in the refrigerator, because it is based on books I have not written yet, on my future royalties, and that is frightening'.

In her nine previous books, her point of view was highly subjective, she usually wrote in the first person singular, and the books revolved around issues from her private domestic existence. It is therefore quite surprising that Orly Castel-Bloom is the author of the first Israeli novel to deal explicitly with the Intifada, the Palestinian uprising.

She began writing it well before the turbulent events, but the news took over and infiltrated her pages. 'It proves that when the cannons roar, the Muses are not necessarily silenced', she says. She manifested her anxiety by training her children how to react if they run into a terrorist, and was pleased that her nine-year-old son immediately dropped to the floor. Although she is not religious at all, she was desperate enough to teach them the prayer of *Shema Israel* ('Hear O Israel, the Lord our God, the Lord is One'), to recite if they encounter a suicide bomber. Jewish Martyrs throughout the ages have cried out these words as they met their deaths.

*Human Parts* follows eight men and women, each representing a different aspect of Israeli life:

- Liat Dubnow and her half-brother Adir Bergson, who are busy with the real estate they inherited from their mother in Tel Aviv. This is Castel-Bloom's tongue-in-cheek comment on modern Israelis as the offspring of great Jewish intellectuals – the historian Dubnow, and the philosopher Bergson – who waddle along in their materialistic, mediocre, petty lives.
- Iris Ventura, a divorced mother of three struggling on her own (Castel-Bloom inserted into Iris' character many of her own experiences with the ex-husband and financial worries due to the divorce).
- The beautiful Tasaru, an Ethiopian immigrant whose dark looks made her a fashion model, and helped her to achieve her greatest dream, to become 'The Lottery Girl' on TV.
- Angelica Gome, whose husband left her following the death of their only son in the army.
- Katy Bet Halachmi, a cleaning lady who wins her five minutes

of fame by appearing on news and TV talk shows as a typical
example of poverty. She's so enchanted by the glow of TV that
she dreams of remaining there by becoming a make-up artist.
She's rescued from her plight only when her husband Boaz, an
unemployed taxi driver, is killed in a terror attack, entitling his
family to a life-long governmental allowance.

- The last protagonist is President Reuven Tekoa, (whose name
  also means 'stuck'), who passes his days and nights paying
  condolence visits to the homes of Israelis killed in attacks, and is
  relieved that his own daughter lives in safe Boston.

They all live on shaky ground, where human parts are scattered
around, and reality becomes chaotic. They all have to deal with the
daily insanity of buses exploding in the streets, where a dash to the
supermarket, or having a cup of coffee with friends, can be fatal.
Castel-Bloom's characteristic irony and sense of humour are at their
best when she describes and analyses Israeli media behaviour:

> In the past, when there was a terror attack, the broadcasters'
> tone would become sombre, and the songs mellow, mostly in
> Hebrew. But since death and terror have become routine, there
> is an unwritten rule, that up to five dead, you continue
> programmes as scheduled, and only from five up do you switch
> down gear to quiet songs, even in English, preferably about the
> fate of Man, such as 'Dust in the Wind'.
>
> From ten dead and up, the radio channels would adopt a
> stricter form, playing Hebrew songs only, such as Korin Allal's 'I
> Have No Other Land', or a new song, realistic and poignant that
> was composed in those terrible days, sung by Yehuda Policker:
> 'Whose Turn is it Next?' And from 20 dead and up ...

'I am a self-appointed Josephus Flavius', says Castel-Bloom, and
feels that she's writing out of the besieged fortress of Massada, from
the blood-covered streets, in order to record and define the events
and map them, as one charts a malignant tumour. 'I'm writing for
future generations, hoping we're not the last one, praying that we
won't end up as a colourful film about an extinct tribe on the
National Geographic television channel'.

## TRANSLATED INTO ENGLISH

Castel-Bloom, O., *Dolly City* [trans. D. Bilu] (London: Loki Books, 1997).

—— *Human Parts* [*Halakim Enoshyim*; trans. D. Bilu (Canada, 2003).

# CHAPTER TWENTY

# Dorit Rabinyan
## (1972– )

# Cinderella's Lost Sandal

Books are piled on the low wooden table, a glass vase crammed with white narcissus, a tiny bottle of aromatic flower essence, and a stethoscope, conspicuous by its incongruity. I wonder whether Dorit Rabinyan is dating a doctor who left the tools of his trade with her, or whether she had been stricken by a sudden attack of hypochondria.

'I bought it for myself about a year and a half ago', she laconically exclaims. At night she inserts the rubber covered hearing plugs into her ears and places the cold metal disk against her exposed chest or naked stomach. 'I like to listen to my heartbeats, or the rumblings of my stomach. It helps me detach and concentrate on myself. You have to block the outside noises in order to hear your inner sounds'. She hands it to me, and with the skill of a clinician guides me to the right spots and inquires: 'Well, how is it?'

The stethoscope has found its way into her novel, *Our Weddings*, a sophisticated version of the Cinderella story, with girls dreaming of marrying a prince, leaving their sandals all over the place, and ending up empty and disappointed, without even a frog to kiss. The parents in the novel, married young, full of love and yearnings, were modelled on the happy marriage of her own parents, 'who have no memories of other beds, no secrets, no suffering'.

Dorit was born in 1972 in Kfar Saba, the eldest daughter of Zion and Yafa Rabinyan, the owners of a small jeans' sewing workshop in southern Tel Aviv; a family rich in love and warmth:

> I grew up in a kind of loving cocoon of parents and brothers and sisters and aunts and grandmothers, my mother was the great sun in the centre and we, the four children, were the four small planets that revolved around her.

Says Rabinyan:

> There is something so wonderful and reassuring about the organism called 'The Family', a multi-limbed, multi-headed creature. It's awful to tear oneself from such a large, warm body, but it is essential for growth. I would very much like to use the 'Me' term, but I can't. It's not accidental that I haven't yet written a novel with a first person singular narrator, only stories told by 'We'.

She remembers a kitchen filled with women, exchanging recipes and love. Five aunts on her mother's side, one aunt on her father's. When one of them was giving birth, Dorit would accompany her grandmother to the maternity ward, stretching her child-frame up into the delivery room window and calling out encouragingly, 'Don't cry, Auntie, it will be all right, the baby will soon emerge'. She stifled her envy when she saw the new mothers kissing the penis of their sons, saying, 'May I be an expiation for your lovely little willie', even swallowing the foreskin after circumcision so that for the rest of their lives they might feel their sons floating inside them.

'My traditional society defined womanhood as poverty, but I have turned it into wealth', she says:

> As a child I was jealous of the preference for boys, then the jealousy became anger and disappointment, but I turned the offence into a source of strength, which produced literature and power. I am a link in a chain of astonishing women in my family. My aunts are overpowering, explosive, large-hearted bundles of energy.

The children of Soli and Iran Azizyan, the protagonists of *Our Weddings*, loved to hear their mother describe their forthcoming nuptials: white dresses, long lace trains, the groom's black suit, champagne and delicatessen. The hypnotic murmur of the story-

telling penetrated the nocturnal dreams of the children – the first-
born son, Maurice, and the daughters, Sophia, Marcelle and Lizzie.
When they grew up the magic worked its spell and grasped their
will like fingers tightening around the throat, they were all afire,
longing to be wed. The girls were drawn to marriage, '... like beach
sandals abandoned on the shore, carried off by the waves. The three
big girls were all married in one year, one after the other, catching
the wedding fever, as if it were a contagious childhood disease ...'
writes Rabinyan in her ornate style. But within the same year they
were all back home, shamefaced, battered and bruised, '... like
seaweed, like sea-shells, like unwanted guests, stunned with grief
and stinking up the house with the scorched smell of their memories'. Sadly, the father sees how his three darling daughters, who
used to giggle as they snuggled up to him, have become disappointed, embittered women.

– *'Did you too grow up on stories of weddings?'*
'Up to the age of 13 or 14 I was the permanent bridesmaid; me and
my cousins were dressed like little brides, and we followed the
bridal train. As charming as it is, it implants a desired goal for an
immature little girl. The bride was pampered and cosseted all day
long, everyone was interested and concerned about her coiffure and
make-up and dress and shoes, and the nice clothes she had packed
for the honeymoon. And for us, the little girls, everything was the
same in miniature, we too were dressed up and prettified like brides.
The wedding was a lighthouse permanently twinkling in the
distance. With no ill intentions – with goodwill and affection – you
are given the message that, "One day, your bridal train will be
carried by other little girls"'.

*Our Weddings* deals with this social conditioning. Maurice, the
eldest – whose admiring mother had taught him that a woman
should smell of garlic from her fingers, milk from her breasts and
myrrh between her legs – passes his time playing cards, visiting pros-
titutes and staring at the naked women hanging on the wall of his
room, for no real woman is good enough for him. Lying on his bed
he fantasies about the woman he will marry, 'And she should have a
big, heavy ass, he thought, and breasts the same size...he might also
drink champagne from one of her bridal slippers, like he saw once
in a Turkish film'.
His sister Sophia, pretty but tired, who loves money, was

crowned the beauty queen of the ORT vocational school, where she learned hairdressing, and achieved the peak of her dreams: a rich husband and a magnificent penthouse in Bat Yam, so high you can see nothing from it. Her youngest sister Lizzie, a man-hunter since her early teens, who exploits the cunning use of alcohol to catch suitors and break their hearts, is married off quickly because of a pregnancy which proves to be imaginary. She comes home from her nights out, rattling on her stiletto heels, wearing beneath her nurse's overcoat a dress with a plunging neckline in which she has been dancing with her lovers, her body blue from the blows of the husband she has betrayed. The middle sister, Marcelle, with the sad eyes and the smiling dimples – like Dorit Rabinyan herself; and, like her, a compulsive reader, who 'shed poems instead of tears' – has a one-sided love for Yoel Hajbi, a senior student at her school:

> Through all those years Marcelle had confused Yoel with the imaginary heroes that her sad eyes cut out of the romances she read ... and she realized that all through the past years she had merely travelled over the road map of the land of love, never in the land itself.

'That's no reason for divorcing, my soul', her mother says in shock, when Marcelle comes back from her honeymoon and announces that she no longer loves Yoel. But the story of Marcelle's marriage is over so quickly that the day of the divorce seems more real than the wedding day.

In her book, Rabinyan is sympathetic towards the broken woman, 'who had resigned her post of mother, packed up all the family's troubles, and withdrew on her own into sorrow's small, private and shut-off chamber', visiting fortune-tellers, graves of the righteous and readers of coffee-cups, trying to understand how the lives of her children had become such a mess. *Our Weddings* is a story of parting: how children part from their childhood, and how difficult it is for mothers, whose whole identity derives from being parents, to relinquish responsibility for their grown-up children.

'In my first novel, *Persian Brides*, there was a very heavy, restrictive, ever-present social injunction that encouraged marriage at an early age', says Rabinyan:

> In *Our Weddings*, the injunction is much more subtle; no one compelled Sophia, Marcelle and Lizzie to accept the first man

who proposed to them, but they did. Since they were children, someone had put them on a train with only one destination. The body speaks to them, cries aloud, imploring them to refuse to marry, but they do not listen to it, for someone cut out the tongue of their will-power.

We are drugged with romantic novels and Turkish films and sayings like, 'Everything will be better when you're married', and we rush panic-stricken towards the wedding-canopy, out of hunger, almost as though it were a children's disease we cannot recover from until we take the marriage vow. We leave the 'We' of the family and move directly to the 'Us' of the couple, without any 'Me' in the middle. I think that on the way from 'We' to 'Us' there has to be a 'Me', otherwise you have no energy for living.

At the age of 22, Dorit married novelist Dov Elboim, whom she met when they were both soldier-journalists on the IDF magazine, *BaMahane* [In Camp]. The marriage lasted two years, 'When you are adolescent, you are allowed to make mistakes, and marriage was one of them. But as soon as I emotionally could, I left'.

*– 'Like Marcelle's mother, who said, "That's no reason for divorcing", did your family try to dissuade you?'*
'They wanted what was best for me, and when they saw how good I felt, they accepted my decision. There were no victims; there was no price. I merely had to reach the point where I could ask my heart what it wanted, and it said, "To get out". It wasn't complicated, there were no children involved, there was no property to split, just the relationship between us, which had passed its expiry date. There was no question of whether I had done right or wrong and when I had corrected my mistake, the family saw at once how I flourished'.

*– 'Did they consider it a failure of your upbringing?'*
'The lighthouse of marriage is only one of a host of glimmering lights. By my decision I broadcast a message to my mother, my aunts and my grandmothers that the fabric from which they had sewn themselves a life, self-determination and joy, was too restricted for me. Today they can see that I'm really choosing other patterns from life's catalogue of costumes, and they're happy for me'.

Her language is elevated, rich, picturesque, sensuous. She lives in a quiet lane off the bohemian Shenkin Street in Tel Aviv, sharing a rented apartment with another woman tenant, just like a couple of students. Only now, it seems, after getting away from her parents and separating from her husband, is she beginning to breathe independently.

'The divorce was the first time I said "I", and the effect on me was hypnotic, intoxicating', she says:

> Maybe I even fell in love with saying 'I' and not being obliged to say 'We'. Along with the pain of separation, it was the beginning of a celebration of the self, of everything embodied in the 'I', independence and freedom and search. A pleasant life focused on my own moods. I do what is good for me at any given moment. I write novels, but my romances today are like short stories. It suits me to move around with a tent on my back. To find a new place every time, to look at the view and then to move on. Eventually, I shall have a permanent home but I'm not yet eager for it.

**– *Aren't you under pressure to have children?'***
'I must first become a whole person before I can give birth'.

On a wall in her study there is an enlarged black and white photograph: the face of a small boy with short hair and sparkling, mischievous eyes. Only at a closer look do you discover that the boy is Dorit.

When she was a little more than two years old, her baby brother was born. There was tremendous joy at the birth of male offspring. But the newborn was ill, blue and coughing. His life was short and difficult. His death, after nine months, left a bleeding wound which 25 years later has not yet healed.

She was moved out of the house when her brother's condition deteriorated and, for many weeks, stayed with her aunts. At his death, she was returned to a house of pain and stillness. She felt obliged to fill the rooms with her presence, to be clamorous enough for two, to fill the place of the absent brother. 'I wanted to occupy the space he had left behind and I became an extra-special, noisy, double Dorit'.

In a house full of scissors and hair dyes and spray and rollers, Dorit would stand in front of the mirror and cut her hair, even to a state of baldness. Her mother would take her to an aunt who was a hairdresser, to try and repair the damage. 'It can be interpreted in all kinds of ways', says Dorit Rabinyan:

> I certainly had the desire to extinguish my femininity and be like my brother, maybe even be the boy who was gone. Up to the age of 14, I was a tomboy, with short hair and bruises on my legs from climbing trees. The transformation occurred when my breasts began to grow.

Dorit Rabinyan preserves the memory of her baby brother in *Our Weddings*, not only in the blue, coughing child of Sophia, but in the twins, Matti and Moni, who were conceived in the aged womb of Iran Azizyan – when her children have already grown up – after the knot the doctor tied in her tubes had come undone:

> For nine whole months Moni and Matti swam together in the amniotic fluid that swarmed with tiny bubbles inside Mama's womb. From bright translucent pipes they grew larger, rolled over, sprouted new limbs, opened and closed their astonished eyes, pressed against the partition between them, and made funny faces at each other. Sometimes they slept back to belly, like spoons, and scratched or kicked when Mama ate something tasty.

But on the day of birth something goes wrong and Paradise is laid waste; the son is stillborn and the daughter becomes a hyperactive child who has to be sent away to an institution. 'A lot of me is deeply invested in Matti', says Dorit Rabinyan. 'Of all the characters in my books, she resembles me the most. When I was writing her I cried, I felt my fingers burning'.

*– 'Were you too a hyperactive child, were you too treated with psychiatric drugs?'*
'Fortunately not: though there were children in the neighbourhood who received that treatment. Especially in the slums, the authorities are too quick to prescribe the drug, as teachers don't have the will and patience to deal with hyperactive children, whose *joie de vivre* is too irrepressible. This horrible drug crushes and blurs your personality'.

We set the interview for noon, but even this was too early for her; she doesn't sleep at night, begins writing after midnight and stops at eight in the morning. Then she disconnects the telephone and sleeps until four in the afternoon:

> Darkness and the fact that the whole world is asleep brings a kind of quietness, and makes time softer, neutralizing the positive vibrations of humanity that abound in daylight. It is easier then to convince myself for several hours that the solitude I must have in order to write is inviolable.

– *'Do you consider seclusion as a sacrifice?'*
'Yes. The world is so tempting, so attractive. I am torn by the temptation to live my life and not write it. In order not to be alone, I have found ways of creating a "We" for myself. There are three of us: Dorit the boss; Dorit the secretary; and Dorit the research assistant. Dorit the boss is the one who writes. She leaves instructions for Dorit the secretary, who takes care of daily matters, and it is the boss who sends Dorit the research assistant to collect data, to sniff around, to verify information. We leave each other notes, make coffee and gossip; sometimes we quarrel when one of us, usually me, wants to close the shop and go out. The other two press her to stop being silly and write'.

– *'What do you mean by "Leave each other notes"?'*
'Real notes: "Hi Dorit, tomorrow do this-and-that. Check whether what we have written is correct. Have a nice day. Yours, Dorit"'.

– *'Does each of the three "Dorits" have a different handwriting? Is it a real split personality?'*
'No', she laughs, 'all the notes are in the same handwriting. The meaningful split is not threefold but between me as a woman and me as a writer. The work is tiring, drudgery, a labour of years, and when the reader receives the book, he has to feel the trickery, the magic. He must not see the heart that suffers, the grubby hands. It's somewhat like Cinderella and the mysterious princess. Cinderella does the hard work and the mysterious princess benefits from the magic, but while she is dancing with the prince her eyes are all the time on the clock, poor thing, such pressure. All the time she knows it can end at any moment. When I go out for the evening, I prefer to leave Dorit the writer at home, she is such a weight, so

depressing, such a thinker, such an observer, she's always detached. Dorit the woman is more frivolous, more of a silly young thing'.

On television guest shows, with her black hair flowing down her shoulders, framing her generous cleavage and bold scarlet lipstick, she is provocative, flaunting her sexuality. She is very different from the hard-working wunderkind who created *Persian Brides*, her first novel, from the stories of her Persian grandmother – which at the age of 22 turned her into a maverick, sold over 80,000 copies, and was translated into English, German, French, Spanish, Italian, Swedish, Greek, Portuguese, Bulgarian, Hungarian, Turkish and Dutch.

Dorit the television personality was light-headed to the point of frivolity, or as she wrote in her book of youthful poems, *Yes, Yes, Yes*, published in 1991:

Under my dress I am only a sweaty, Asiatic chick, / flighty and licking my lips as a come-on / an empty-headed female whose cheap scent / is sweet as the odour of garbage.

When I mention her book of poems, she flinches as though it were a can of worms. 'That is one of my adolescent stupidities', she says. Despite its quality, she tries to disown it, claiming that it is immature, but it seems that what really embarrasses her, are some of the more daring, outspoken poems.

– *'Your novels have the fragrance of Persia, whereas your poetry is of bohemian Tel Aviv, and very, very sexy'.*
'I wrote them when I was 16 to 18, searching for an identity and wishing to cut myself off from the tribe I belonged to. The whole idea was to skip from one image of myself to another, to be reflected in all kinds of mirrors, to present an impression of the "I". At 15 I was a Punk, I frequented the Tel Aviv nightclubs, my hair spiky with gel, in black clothes, listening to the depressive music of Nick Cave. Within half a year I had changed completely, I had become a Freak, my dresses transparent, bought at a Flea Market, singing of love and peace. I needed to devote myself to a new "We", the opposite of the other "We" I grew with. I always needed to be a part of the herd, a member of some gang'.

She is an ardent reader, 'Like a fresh student in a class of adults, devouring books. The moment I finish one, I start from the top, examining how the author achieved the magic, where he has hidden the rabbit'. She says if she were not a writer, she would burst at the seams:

> I don't know anyone, certainly not myself, who would sit and write for eight hours a day, if it were not for some lack, something broken in his life. History of art proves that emotional confusion and a crisis of values are a prerequisite for creation. I create not out of abundance but out of broken worlds.

– *'What is so broken about your world? You grew up in a big, loving family'*.
'There was a kind of weakness, when the home confronted the street. If I had not been the daughter of immigrants, if I were not aware of the gap between Ispahan and Kfar Saba, the tension between what my parents expected to find here and what they found, I would probably not have become a writer. That is the pit out of which I write. I was aware of the tentativeness, the dismay, the insecurity of mothers who moved around among high people and complicated words, smiling the smile of broken-hearted immigrants, their mouths stuffed with saliva and a foreign accent. There seems to have been a tremour in the voice, a shaking in the hand that held me, that I absorbed from signs, overt and covert, and that broke my heart, leaving me with a respect for weakness and a desire for greater strength, for a sense of belonging'.

– *'Is that why you developed such an amazing control of Hebrew?'*
'I strove to know Hebrew perfectly, to tame it to perform tricks, to transform it into beauty, which is the only possible way to overcome the pain. I was a child who had to read everything, even the contents on food packages. When I began to be bored with the children's library, and was still forbidden to enter the adults', my mother joined the library and told the librarian that the little girl, me, would take home the books for her. I was proud that Mother was deceiving the authorities on my behalf, so that I could satisfy a hunger that had woken in me'.

On her refrigerator there were magnets with pictures of rabbis. It's just a joke, she said, but admitted she was living between two worlds. 'I visit a psychologist, who provides me with the best that the West has to offer, and at the same time I believe that my aunt has power to ward off the Evil Eye'.

*– 'Do you classify yourself as a Sephardi writer?'*
'I am in the middle, neither here nor there. I have a sense of comradeship with people like me, who were caressed by the same accent when they were babies, who had the same taste on their tongues. I would like to believe that the personal creativity of Sephardi artists, will strengthen girls like Sophia, Marcelle and Lizzie, not to be stuck where the possibilities are restricted and boldness is stifled, and will power is stunted'.

Sometimes she imagines her characters living in a three-storey house, sitting there in the evening, smoking, cracking sunflower seeds, gossiping about her. 'They tell stories about me. "Why is she sad? Why is she always so sad?" But I shall always write about immigrants, about mobility; about the gap between what you wish for, and what you get'.

## TRANSLATED INTO ENGLISH

Rabinyan, D., *Persian Brides* [*Simtat Hashkediot Be'omrijan*; trans. Y. Lotan] (Edinburgh: Cannongate Publishing/New York: Braziler Publishing, 1997).
—— *Our Weddings* [*Hachatunot Shelanu*; trans. Y. Lotan] (London: Bloomsbury Publishing, 2001/New York: Random House, 2002).